D1096343

RESTAURANT LÉA LINSTER
ROUTE DE LUXEMBOURG 17
L-5752 FRISANGE
FOR RESERVATION PLEASE CALL: 00352 23 66 84 11

LËTZEBURGER KASCHTHAUS
ROUTE DE BETTENBOURG 4
L-3333 HELLANGE
FOR RESERVATION PLEASE CALL: 00352 51 65 73

OR VISIT OUR WEB SITE: WWW.LEALINSTER.LU

LÉA LINSTER

Best of
LEA LINSTER
CUISINIÈRE

Edited and approved by Léa Linster

Photographs by Susie Knoll and Guy Hoffmann
Texts by Simone van de Voort
Translated by Chip Browder

Foreword by Paul Bocuse

I wish to give thanks to the following people: Paul Bocuse, Fredy Girardet, Pierre Troisgros, Joël Robuchon and Alfred Biolek for all that they have taught me over the years; my father for talent and my mother for stamina; Barbara Fischer Fürwentsches and Ernst-Dieter Wiesner for their financial advice; the "saint-paul Luxembourg" printers employees; my friends Béatrice Cointreau, Christine Ferber, Burgunde Uhlig, Susanne Mersmann, Jil Mercedes, Renate Seherra, Dietlind Davis, Doris Montornes, and Nathalie Maillet for their love and support; my doctor Anna-Louise Rinneberg; Claude Peiffer of Villeroy & Boch; the Munich team Susie Knoll, her husband, and Paul Zentner for artistic direction; Chip Browder for his translation; Simone van de Voort for the production of the book and to my staff with Hákon Már Örvarsson. Of course my strongest supporters are at home: Thank you Louis and Sam for your enthusiasm and your patience.

CONTENTS

FOREWORD

Colorful and outspoken, Léa Linster has commanded respect since her youth in the traditionally very masculine profession of Chef de Cuisine. Initially, however, there was nothing to indicate that she was destined for the profession of chef. She was diligently attending the University of Law, when the premature death of her father obliged her to change her focus. She succeeded her parents and grandparents who were, in their time, forerunners of the "drugstores of the sixties", simultaneously performing as bakers and pastry chefs, operating a combination café, restaurant and gas station.

Léa chose to travel a path that is not easy for a woman, constantly fighting to make a name for herself. To achieve this, she completed training courses in the great houses, such as at Fredy Girardet in Crissier. More importantly, she rapidly obtained her "Brevet de Maitrise de Cuisinier". Her next step was to enroll as a competitor in the second contest of "Bocuse d'Or" in 1989, from which she left as champion with her superb dish "Saddle of lamb in Potato Crust".

Léa Linster has succeeded in establishing a name for herself, one which will become increasingly well known the world over. Supported in her efforts by her staff, she has managed in a few years to elevate the cuisine of her country to among the most prized internationally. Under the admiring eye of her son Louis, she leads a life of purpose, leaving nothing to chance. Our Léa is and will continue to be a woman of masterful accomplishment, who has found the time to put together a new book, sharing with us her secrets for simple yet elegant dishes.

This work is guaranteed to be a success and will undoubtedly add to her long list of awards. It was certainly no accident that she chose the printing company "saint-paul Luxembourg" to print this book. I am confident that this edition will add to Léa Linster's considerable renown. This is what I sincerely wish for Léa, because she has earned it. And as she likes to say:

«*Cuisine de femme ou cuisine d'homme, il n'y en a qu'une seule, c'est la bonne!*»
"Woman's cooking or man's cooking, there is only one - the good one!"

Paul Bocuse

DEAR READER,

The desire of certain customers and friends to enjoy one of my dishes in their own home that they had eaten years before, prompted me to write this book. Actually, sometimes I no longer knew exactly how I had made some of those dishes, and I had not written down any of the recipes. Thus after more than twenty years of cooking, I thought that it was really time to write a book containing all of my favorite recipes, not only for you, but also for me, to circumvent new lapses of memory.

In this book I have assembled the best recipes presented in my two restaurants. The recipes approach as much as possible the original preparation, with some adaptations that are necessary for the home kitchen. Certainly, some recipes will seem too long or complicated. A word of advice: take only what you feel are the best and most useful techniques and suggestions from my recipes. There is a beginning to everything. I, too, began by cooking simply, by brewing coffee and making pasta for my parents. As I advanced, pre-packaged soups followed. Gradually I improved upon them. Finally, when I was ready, I completely abandoned the packages and made soups from beginning to end according to my taste.

Do not be afraid of new recipes. Start with simple dishes, advance slowly, and take risks only when you feel comfortable with a preparation. For example, if you know how to cook a steak well, you can try a new sauce or a different side dish. There are also dishes that are easy to learn, are treats unto themselves and, in the end, can save an entire meal. I am thinking in particular of my crème brûlée, with which the success of your meal will be guaranteed.

Always remember that it is absolutely essential to use only the freshest products of the highest quality. This is the basis of my cooking. You will recognize quality products by their taste: honest, ripe, untainted, and genuine. If you work with such products you will not need tricks to succeed. The principal ingredient of a dish should be able to stand on its own. The sauce and the garnishes serve only to highlight the characteristics of the main ingredient. Good cooking is being able to emphasize the merits of each component!

Finally, I would like to give you a last bit of advice. Always take pleasure in and lavish love on your efforts because, if you cook for someone you love and if you love what you cook, all will be well!

The creation and the making of "Best of Léa Linster" has given me enormous pleasure. I wish the same for you in your discovery of it.

Yours sincerely,

Lea Linster

MY ROLLS
MES PETITS PAINS

Makes about 40 to 50
Rest period: 1 night,
the following day 3 hours

Leaven:
$^1/_4$ ounce (5 g) fresh baker's yeast
1 $^1/_2$ cups (300 ml) cold water
1 $^3/_4$ - 2 cups (250 g bread flour, sifted

Dough:
5 $^1/_2$ - 6 cups (750 g) bread flour, sifted
$^1/_3$ ounce (10 g) fresh baker's yeast
1 $^1/_2$ cups (300 ml) warm water
1 heaping tablespoon (18 g) fine sea salt
flour for the work surface

Note:
The rolls freeze very well. Reduce the cooking time by 5 minutes, let them cool, and freeze them. Right before serving, finish baking them in a preheated 500°F (250°C) oven for 8 to 10 minutes.

Leaven:
Crumble the yeast into a bowl. Reduce to a smooth cream with 2 tablespoons of cold water. Incorporate the remaining water. Add the flour and mix the whole in order to obtain a smooth mixture. Cover the leaven with plastic wrap and let it rest at room temperature (68°F / 20°C) at least 8 hours, preferably 24 hours.

Dough:
In the bowl of an electric mixer put the flour, crumbled yeast, leaven, and water. With the hook attachment knead at high speed for 10 to 12 minutes until the dough is quite smooth and firm. Add the salt and continue to knead approximately 2 minutes so that the dough is detached from the bowl and becomes flexible.

Put the dough on a lightly floured work surface and form into a ball. Flour it and cover it with a damp cloth. Let rest for 2 hours at room temperature.

For the rolls:
Divide the dough into four pieces, then roll each piece into a Cylinder from 1 - 1$^1/_2$ inches (3 to 4 cm) in diameter and cut into small pieces to obtain portions of dough around 1$^1/_2$ ounces (35 to 40 g) each. Work each piece, while working it as little as possible, into rolls from 3 to 4 inches (8 to 10 cm) in length with pointed ends. Lay out the rolls on a baking sheet lined with parchment paper, spacing them an inch (2$^1/_2$ cm) or so apart. Cover them with a damp linen towel and let them double in volume at room temperature (approximately 50 minutes), sheltered from drafts within a turned-off oven.

After removing the rolls, preheat the oven to 500°F (250°C). Lightly dust the rolls with flour at the time of baking and make a lengthwise incision in them with a small, well-sharpened knife or a razor blade. Place a heat-resistant bowl, filled with hot water, on the floor of the oven. At the same time, place the baking pan back into the oven and let the rolls bake for 20 to 25 minutes until they are golden and crusty. Let cool slightly on wire racks and serve while still warm, with good butter.

SOUPS AND STEWS

SOUPES ET POTAGES

VICHYSSOISE
SOUPE FROIDE AU POIREAUX ET POMMES DE TERRES

Serves 6 to 8

Soup:
2 large leeks (white parts only)
2 potatoes of average size
(approximately 13 ounces, 400 g)
2 tablespoons (30 g) butter
1 3/4 quarts (1 3/4 liters)
chicken broth or stock (p. 172)
fine sea salt
1 cup (200 g) heavy cream
1/2 cup (100 g) crème fraîche

Garnish:
1 leek
(white and light green parts only)
fine sea salt
1 bunch fresh chives, finely minced

Soup:
Clean the leek whites, wash, drain and cut them into thin slices. Peel the potatoes, wash and drain them, and chop them in small cubes. Heat the butter in a large pan, add the leek whites and return to medium heat for a few minutes. Add the potatoes; moisten with the chicken broth, salt lightly. Bring to the boil and let cook at a slow boil for 25 minutes.

Purée the soup with an immersion blender or in a food processor. Add the heavy cream and crème fraîche, and continue to blend until the soup is quite smooth. Bring back to the boil for a moment and then pass through a sieve.
Let cool at least 2 to 3 hours in the refrigerator.

Garnish:
Clean the leek, split it lengthwise, and wash and drain it. Cut the leek diagonally into diamond-shaped pieces 1/2 - 3/4 inches (1-2 cm). Blanch the pieces in boiling salted water for 1 minute. Shock them in ice water, drain them and dry them on absorbent paper towels.

Before serving, correct the seasoning of the soup. If the consistency of soup is too thick, add a little more heavy cream or milk. Blend the soup again to make it foam and pour it into chilled bowls or soup plates. Garnish it with the blanched leek pieces and chives.

Note:
Vichyssoise is traditionally served cold, but it is also good served hot.

CHILLED TOMATO SOUP WITH FRESH GOAT CHEESE AND MINT

SOUPE DE TOMATES GLACÉE AU CHÈVRE FRAIS ET À LA MENTHE

Serves 4

Soup:

*2 pounds (1 kg) ripe
but firm tomatoes
(preferably Roma tomatoes)
1 teaspoon sugar
fine sea salt
6 - 8 tablespoons cider vinegar
1 pinch Cayenne pepper*

Garnish:

*5 ounces (150 g) soft
mild goat cheese
2 tablespoons minced
fresh mint leaves
coarsely ground black pepper
extra-virgin olive oil*

Soup:

Wash the tomatoes, remove the cores and cut the tomatoes into large pieces. Purée the pieces well with an immersion blender. Then pass the mixture through a sieve while pressing down firmly to obtain the maximum amount of flesh (without skin or seeds). Alternatively, pass through the fine blade of a food mill. Put the purée in a bowl, season with salt, the vinegar to taste and a little Cayenne pepper and let it marinate at least 2 hours in the refrigerator.

Garnish and assembly:

Before serving the chilled soup, check the seasoning, blend it again and pour it into cold bowls or glasses. Garnished with 1 or 2 tablespoons of goat cheese, some minced mint leaves and coarse pepper to taste. Drizzle with olive oil and serve.

CREAM OF CELERIAC
CRÈME DE CÉLERY-RAVE

Serves 4

Cream:
1 small celery root (celeriac)
or a half of a large one
(approximately 1 1/4 pounds, 600 g)
2 - 3 tablespoons olive oil
2 1/4 cups (1/2 liter) chicken broth
or stock (p. 172)
1 - 1 1/4 cups (250 g) heavy cream
1 cup (1/4 liter) full-fat milk
fine sea salt
freshly ground pepper
a few drops fresh lemon juice

Garnish:
2 celery stalks
fine sea salt

For serving:
2 tablespoons whipped cream
parsley oil (p. 169)
or extra-virgin olive oil
a few celery leaves

Cream:

Peel the celeriac, wash and cut it into small cubes. Heat the cubes for 3 to 4 minutes in olive oil over a low heat in a saucepan. Add the chicken broth or stock and let it simmer for 15 to 20 minutes until the celeriac is very tender. After cooking, add the cream and milk and bring to the boil. Remove from the heat. Purée with an immersion blender or in a food processor until the soup becomes a smooth and consistent cream. Pass it through a sieve and season with salt, pepper, and a few drops of lemon juice.

Garnish:

Using a vegetable peeler, peel the celery stalks. Cut in fine slices lengthwise, then in very small cubes. Blanch the cubes in boiling salted water, shock them in ice water, drain and dry them between two absorbent paper towels.

To serve:

Divide the cubes among four hot bowls or soup plates. Heat the celery cream, check the seasoning, add the whipped cream, blend to make it foam and pour it in the bowls. Garnish with a drizzle of parsley oil or olive oil and some celery leaves.

CREAM OF PUMPKIN SOUP WITH SMALL BUTTERED CROÛTONS

CRÈME AU POTIRON, PETITS CROÛTONS AU BEURRE

Serves 4

Croûtons:
2 slices white sandwich bread
(preferably homemade)
2 - 3 tablespoons (30 - 40 g)
clarified butter (p. 169)

Cream:
11 - 12 ounces (350 g)
fresh pumpkin pulp
1 small onion
2 - 3 tablespoons (40 g) butter
3 cups ($^3/_4$ liter)
chicken broth or stock (p. 172)
1 $^1/_4$ cups (250 g) heavy cream
fine sea salt
1 pinch ground cinnamon
freshly ground pepper

For Serving:
4 tablespoons of whipped cream

Croûtons:
Preheat the oven to 300°F (150°C).

Remove the crust from the slices of sandwich bread. With a serrated-edged knife, cut the slices horizontally at least once, preferably twice to obtain very thin bread slices (cutting is easier if the bread slices are slightly frozen). Cut the slices in sticks between $^1/_6$ and $^1/_4$ inch (4 mm) in stripes, then into very small regular cubes.

Melt the clarified butter in a frying pan, add the bread cubes, mix well with butter and spread them out on a parchment paper lined baking sheet. Put the croûtons in the oven and allow them to color for approximately 15 to 20 minutes. Take them out of the oven and let them drain on absorbent paper towels.

Cream:
Cut the pumpkin pulp into 1 inch (2 - 3 cm) pieces. Peel the onion. Halve and thinly slice it. Place the onion in the butter in a pot. Add the pieces of pumpkin, salt lightly, and cover with chicken broth or stock (approximately 1 cup, $^1/_4$ liter). Cover and cook 15 to 20 minutes over low heat until the pumpkin is tender. Add the cream, cook 10 minutes longer, and then purée with an immersion blender or in a food processor. Separately heat the remaining chicken broth or stock and add little by little to the pumpkin purée until a fairly thick cream is obtained. Blend again, pass through a sieve, and season with salt, pepper and cinnamon to taste.

To serve:
Heat the pumpkin cream, divide it into 4 hot soup plates and garnish with a tablespoon of whipped cream and croûtons. Serve at once.

CREAM OF ONION SOUP WITH RIESLING
VELOUTÉ D'OIGNONS AU RIESLING

Serves 4

Soup:

4 medium sized onions,
preferably white
4 tablespoons (60 g) butter
$^1/_4$ cup (40 g) fine wheat semolina
1 cup ($^1/_4$ liter) Riesling
(dry white wine)
3 cups ($^3/_4$ liter) chicken broth
or stock (p. 172)
$^3/_4$ cup (150 g) heavy cream
2 egg yolks
3 ounces (80 g) freshly and finely
grated Parmigiano-Reggiano cheese
fine sea salt
freshly ground pepper
1 pinch freshly grated nutmeg

Garnish:

4 thin slices of baguette
1 ounce (30 g) freshly shredded
Gruyère cheese (Swiss cheese)
2 tablespoons finely
minced fresh chives

Soup:

Peel the onions, quarter, and slice into thin slices. Melt the butter in a large pan, add the onion and heat at low heat for a few minutes while turning the slices regularly. Sprinkle on the semolina and stir well. Pour in the Riesling and then the chicken broth or stock. Bring to the boil and let cook 20 to 25 minutes, stirring from time to time, until the onions are very tender.

Combine well the heavy cream, egg yolks, and Parmigiano-Reggiano in a bowl. Remove the soup from the heat, pour in the egg yolk mixture while whisking constantly. Place the soup over low heat, without boiling, until it thickens. Season with salt, pepper and nutmeg to taste.

Garnish:

Turn on the broiler and toast the baguette slices on both sides. Place the slices side by side on a broiling pan and sprinkle evenly with the shredded Gruyère. Place under the broiler again until the cheese is bubbly and slightly browned.

Divide the soup among four hot bowls or soup plates. Garnish with the chives and a slice of toasted baguette. Serve at once.

BEEF CONSOMMÉ WITH PORCINI
CONSOMMÉ DE BŒUF AUX CÈPES

Serves 6 to 8

Consommé:

3/4 pound (400 g) lean beef
1 small onion
1 carrot
1 stalk celery
fine sea salt
1 egg white, slightly beaten
a few ice cubes
1 1/2 - 2 quarts (1,5 - 2 liters)
rich beef broth or stock (preferably
homemade, pot au feu p.108),
well degreased and cold
2 tomatoes
1 bay leaf
5 black peppercorns
1 fresh thyme sprig
5 parsley sprigs
dry sherry to taste
cheesecloth or muslin

Garnish:

4-5 fresh porcini mushrooms
(cèpes) of average size

Consommé:

Cut the meat into 1 inch (3 cm) pieces. Peel the onion, carrot and celery and cut into large cubes. Pass the meat and vegetables through a meat grinder fitted with a medium blade.

Lightly salt the chopped meat and vegetable mixture and mix well with the egg white and the ice cubes. Put the clarification (meat-vegetable mixture) in a large pot and pour in the beef broth. Cut the tomatoes into small pieces and add them with the bay leaf, peppercorns, thyme, and parsley to the liquid. While whisking to prevent the meat and egg white from coagulating, bring the mixture to a boil over medium heat. As soon as the broth is hot, stop whisking. Reduce the heat and continue to cook at barely a simmer for a good hour. Avoid boiling, so that the soup becomes quite clear.

When the liquid becomes clear, strain it through a fine sieve covered with a double thickness of wet cheesecloth, disturbing the sediment as little as possible. Correct the seasoning and flavor it with a little dry sherry to taste.

Garnish:

Clean the mushrooms, halve them, and then cut into thin slices. Heat a ladleful of consommé in a small saucepan and poach the porcini slices for a few seconds. Drain them.

To serve:

Heat 6 to 8 espresso cups or small bowls. Divide the soup among them and garnish with a few slices of porcini. Serve at once.

CREAMY WHITE BEAN SOUP WITH BLACK TRUFFLES
CRÈME AUX COCOS BLANCS ET AUX TRUFFES

Serves 4 to 6

Soup:

6 - 7 ounces (200 g)
dried white beans
4 - 5 cups (1,2 liters)
chicken broth or stock (p. 172)
3/4 - 1 cup (200 g) heavy cream
3/4 - 1 cup (200 ml) whole milk
fine sea salt
freshly ground pepper

For Serving:

4 tablespoons whipped cream
1 small fresh black truffle,
well cleaned
a few sprigs of chervil

Soup:

Rinse the beans several times under cold water. Drain them and put them in a pot. Cover with 4 cups (1 liter) of chicken broth or stock and cook the beans over low heat for 1 to $1^1/_2$ hours until they are quite tender.

Blend soup with an immersion blender or in a food processor and pass it through a sieve. Add the cream and milk, and process again to obtain a smooth and consistent cream. Bring to the simmer while stirring constantly and season with salt and pepper. If the cream is too thick, thin it with a little hot chicken broth or stock.

To serve:

Heat the soup, add the whipped cream, blend to make it foam and distribute it in hot bowls or soup plates. Shave the truffle over the plates in very fine slices, garnish with a sprig of chervil and serve.

Note:

With this creamy white bean soup, I serve my rolls (p. 15) still warm.

"BOUNESCHLUPP" LUXEMBURGER STEW WITH GREEN BEANS

«BOUNESCHLUPP» POTAGE LUXEMBOURGEOIS

Serves 8

Stew:

2 ¼ pounds (1 kg)
green beans, not too thin
7 ounces (200 g) celery root
(celeriac)
3 medium potatoes
2 medium onions
1 small leek
sea salt
3 tablespoons (50 g) butter
2 tablespoons flour
freshly ground pepper
³/4 cup (150 g) crème fraîche
or sour cream

Garnish:

13 ounces (400 g) smoked
bacon in one piece
4 uncooked pork sausages
(for example: polish kielbasa)

Stew:

String the beans, wash them and cut into pieces ¹/2 - ³/4 inches (1-2 cm) long. Peel the celery root and the potatoes, wash and cut them into ¹/2 inch (1 cm) cubes. Reserve the potatoes in cold water. Peel the onions, halve, and then dice. Clean the leek, wash and drain it, and slice into ¹/2 inch (1 cm) pieces.

Put all of the vegetables, except the potatoes, in a pot, cover with 2 ¹/4 quarts (2 liters) water, salt lightly and cook over medium heat 15 to 20 minutes. Drain the potatoes, add them to the Stew, and continue cooking until the potatoes are tender (approximately 10 minutes).

Melt the butter in a pan and add the flour. With a whisk, vigorously stir over high heat to obtain a white roux. Gradually add a little of the stew broth while whisking constantly. Add as much broth as necessary to make a creamy sauce. Let cook a few minutes over low heat. Pass the sauce through a sieve into the stew and combine well with the vegetables.

Bring to the boil, remove from the heat, season with salt and pepper and divide the stew among large, hot stew bowls. Garnish with a good tablespoon of crème fraîche or sour cream. Serve accompanied by the sausages and cooked bacon (or either one could be used alone, depending on your taste).

Garnish:

Put the smoked bacon in a pan with cold water, do not salt, bring to the boil and cook for a good hour, until the pork rind can be easily removed. Remove the pork from the pan, cut into slices, and then into ¹/4 inch (1 cm) sticks. Serve hot with the stew.

Put the sausages in boiling unsalted water, remove the pan from the heat and let the sausages poach in the hot water for 20 minutes. To serve, take the sausages from the water, slice thinly and serve with the stew while still hot.

SALADS AND APPETIZERS
SALADES ET ENTRÉES FROIDES

STUFFED EGGS
ŒUFS FARCIS

Serves 4

Eggs:
6 extra fresh eggs
sea salt
3 - 4 tablespoons mayonnaise
(p. 168)
$^{1}/_{4}$ - $^{1}/_{2}$ teaspoon Dijon mustard
1 teaspoon finely chopped
fresh chervil
1 tablespoon finely minced
fresh chives
1 pinch Cayenne pepper
a few drops fresh lemon juice

Garnish:
2 small radishes
several blades of chives (optional)

Eggs:

Place the eggs in cold, salted water. Bring to the boil and cook for 8 to 10 minutes, or until hard-boiled. Shock with cold water, drain and let them cool. Peel the hard-boiled eggs and cut in half lengthwise. Remove the egg yolks delicately, without breaking the white.

Crush the egg yolks in a mortar. Bit by bit, add the mayonnaise and the mustard to the mortar and mix until a smooth cream is obtained. Add chervil and chive and season with salt, Cayenne pepper and a little lemon juice to taste.

To serve:

Using a pastry or icing bag provided with a grooved tip, pipe the cream of egg yolks to nicely fill the halves of egg whites. Clean the radishes. Wash and cut or shave them in very thin slices. Garnish the eggs with one or two slices of radish and the chives.

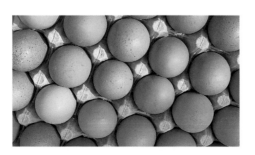

SALMON TARTAR WITH THREE GARNISHES
TATARE DE SAUMON ET SES TROIS GARNITURES

Serves 4

Vodka cream:
4 tablespoons crème fraîche
or sour cream
2 tablespoons whipped cream
fine sea salt
a few drops fresh lemon juice
2 tablespoons (20 ml) vodka

Garnishes:
a small amount of Japanese
seaweed (2 g) (Fueru Wakame)
3 1/2 ounces (100 g)
small raw shrimp
a few drops fresh lemon juice
extra-virgin olive oil
4 - 6 excellent oysters
Sevruga caviar (approximately
1 teaspoon per person)

Tartar:
1 pound (400 g) very fresh wild
salmon fillet, without skin
1 - 2 small shallots
4 tablespoons extra-virgin olive oil
fine sea salt
freshly ground pepper
juice of half a lemon
1 - 2 tablespoons finely
minced chives

Vodka Cream:
Combine crème fraîche or sour cream and whipped cream, and season with salt, vodka, and few drops of lemon juice to taste. Keep the cream refrigerated until ready to use.

Garnishes:
Put the seaweed in a small pan with a little water. Bring to the boil, take off the heat, and let the seaweed steep until plumped up. Drain and chop it finely.
Peel the shrimp, cut in very small pieces and mix with the seaweed. Season with a little lemon juice and olive oil. Open the oysters, put them in a strainer to drain well, and finely chop. Reserve everything in the refrigerator.

Tartar:
Rinse the salmon fillet in cold water, dry it and carefully remove all the gray skin and fat. Cut the salmon, initially in fine slices, then in thin strips, and finally in very small cubes. Put the cubes in a bowl and put that on an ice bath so that the tartar remains quite fresh.

Peel the shallot, slice into two and finely mince. Mix the tartar with the shallots, olive oil, salt and pepper, and the lemon juice. Adjust the seasoning, add the chives, and combine well.

To serve:
Using a small, round form or pastry cutter, form three portions of tartar (1 to 2 tablespoons each) on each cold plate. Top each with one of the garnishes of chopped shrimp and seaweed, oysters, or caviar to your taste. Pass the vodka cream separately.

TERRINE OF DUCK FOIE GRAS
TERRINE DE FOIE GRAS DE CANARD

Makes about 1 3/4 pounds (800 g)

Terrine:

*(to be prepared at least
3 days in advance)*
*2 fresh duck foie gras (each about
1 1/2 pounds, 500 - 600 g)*
3/4 tablespoon (12 g) fine sea salt
*1 teaspoon (2 g) ground
white pepper*
*1 1/2 tablespoons (20 ml)
Armagnac*
*1 1/2 tablespoons (20 ml)
Ruby Port*
*3 tablespoons (40 ml) Sauternes
or another sweet dessert wine*
terrine mold with a 5-cup capacity

For serving:

fleur de sel or coarse sea salt
coarsely ground black pepper
*farmhouse (country-style)
white bread*

Terrine:

Leave the lobes of foie gras at room temperature for 1 to 2 hours before cleaning them. To clean, separate the two lobes of each liver by gently pulling them apart. With a small knife carefully dig into the middle of each lobe, slipping the vein under the knife tip and pulling it out. Gently pull out any other veins (especially the largest), and cut out all traces of blood and gall. Turn over the lobes. Eliminate the thin membrane/skin that covers them. To determine the seasoning, weigh the cleaned lobes. Use 1 tablespoon of salt and 1 teaspoon of pepper per every 2 1/4 pounds (1 kg) of liver. Place the lobes side by side in one layer in a large dish. Salt and pepper them evenly on both sides then sprinkle with Armagnac, Port, and Sauternes. Turn the lobes one time, cover them with plastic wrap and let them macerate in the refrigerator at least 8 to 12 hours or overnight. The following day, let the livers warm up slightly at room temperature before putting them in the terrine mold. Preheat the oven to 250°F (120°C).

First place the large lobes, smooth part (skin side) down, into the mold and cover them with the small lobes, smooth side up, pressing well to avoid air pockets. Place the mold in a larger heatproof dish and fill the larger dish with cold water to within 1 inch (2 cm) of the top edge of the mold. Place the mold and its water bath in the preheated oven and let it cook for 45 minutes or until the internal temperature reaches 115°F (50°C), so that the livers are just warm in the middle. Remove the mold in the water bath from the oven and let it set a little. Take the terrine out of the water bath, place it on a plate to catch any drippings, and compress the liver by placing a small cardboard the same size as the interior of the mold, wrapped in plastic wrap, on top of the liver and placing a weight on it. (The weight should be between 3/4 and 1 pound, 300 to 400 g, for example: a package of butter). Let the terrine firm up overnight in the refrigerator.

The following day, remove the board and collect (scrape) the yellow fat from the top of the terrine and the plate. Melt it over low heat, pass it through a fine sieve and let it cool almost completely. Just before the fat solidifies, pour it uniformly over the surface of the terrine to seal it. Place the terrine in the refrigerator and wait at least 1 day, preferably 2 to 3 days, before serving the foie gras.

To serve:

Run a small knife around the edges of the mold to loosen the terrine. Plunge the bottom of the mold in very hot water to detach the bottom of the terrine, and unmold the terrine on a cutting board. To serve, cut the terrine of foie gras with a sharp knife that has been dipped in hot water into slices about 1/2 inch (1 1/2 cm) thick.
Serve each slice sprinkled with coarsely ground pepper and fleur de sel, accompanied by toasted slices of farmhouse bread.

If you wish, you can serve the foie gras garnished with a purée of artichoke bottoms or a purée of red beets (p. 116).

WARM LOBSTER SALAD WITH TARRAGON SAUCE
SALADE TIÈDE DE HOMARD, SAUCE À L'ESTRAGON

Serves 4

Sauce:
1 ripe but firm tomato
2 tablespoons fresh tarragon leaves
4 tablespoons mayonnaise
(p. 168)
¹/₄ cup (60 ml) shrimp stock
(p. 171)
fine sea salt
1 pinch Cayenne pepper
a few drops fresh lemon juice

Lobsters:
1 organic or unwaxed orange
¹/₄ cup (heaping, 60 g)
coarse sea salt
¹/₄ cup (20 g) dried fennel seeds
2 live lobsters, 1 ¹/₄ - 1 ¹/₂ pound
(500 - 600 g) each

To serve:
6 ounces (150 g, 3 large handfuls)
mixed salad greens
4 tablespoons elegant vinaigrette
(p. 168)
a few chervil sprigs

Sauce:

Remove the core of the tomato. Plunge the tomato into boiling water for 20 seconds, shock with cold water, peel, and cut into quarters. Remove the seeds and cut the quarters into very small cubes. Mince the tarragon fine. Mix the mayonnaise with the shrimp stock and add the minced tarragon and the tomato cubes. Season with salt, Cayenne pepper and lemon juice to taste.

Lobsters:

Prepare the cooking water for the lobster: Using a vegetable peeler or a zester, remove the zest/rind (outer orange part of the skin) of the orange without any of the bitter white pith underneath. Blanch the zest for a few seconds in boiling water. Drain. In a pot, bring to a boil 1 ¹/₂ gallons (6 l) of water, salt, the fennel seed and the blanched orange zest. When the water is at the boil, plunge in one of the two lobsters and let it cook at a slow boil for 4 to 5 minutes. Remove it and let it rest it at least 3 minutes before shelling it. Cook the second lobster in the same way.

Remove the claws and the tails of the lobsters while they are still warm. Using the back of a large knife, a nutcracker, and/or lobster shears, delicately break the claws and the claw joints without damaging the flesh, and shell them. Divide the tails in two lengthwise, remove the intestinal vein, and remove the flesh from the body cavities. Cut the lobster flesh (except the claws) into 1 inch (2 cm) pieces, and keep them covered so that the flesh stays warm.

To serve:

Pick over the salad greens, tear into small pieces, wash and dry them. Toss the leaves with the vinaigrette and arrange in a bouquet in the center of four plates. Drizzle a generous amount of the tarragon sauce around the salad and arrange the warm pieces of lobster (a half lobster per person) in such a way as to reconstruct the shape of the lobster tail. Lay out the claws in place of the head of the lobster. Garnish the plates with some chervil sprigs and serve immediately.

For additional garnishes use quartered, cooked artichoke bottoms and cooked green beans.

CHICKEN ASPIC WITH DUCK FOIE GRAS
GELÉE DE POULETTE AU FOIE GRAS DE CANARD

Serves 8 to 10

Aspic:
3 ¹/₄ cups (700 ml) very clear
chicken stock (p. 172)
¹/₄ cup (50 ml) dry white wine
(Riesling)
fine sea salt
balsamic vinegar
Madeira
a few drops Truffle juice
(obtainable at fine food stores)
2 envelopes (¹/₄ ounce each)
gelatin or 8 sheets of gelatin
(2 g each)

Garnish:
2 large boneless chicken breast
halves, skin on
fine sea salt
freshly ground pepper
1 - 2 tablespoons (20 g) butter
1 teaspoon balsamic vinegar
1 tablespoon finely
minced tarragon leaves
6 slices foie gras terrine,
each ¹/₂ inch (1 ¹/₂ cm) thick,
around 3 ounces/80 g (p. 40)
terrine mold with a 5-cup capacity

For serving:
fleur de sel or coarse sea salt
coarsely ground black pepper
farmhouse (country-style)
white bread

Aspic:

Heat the chicken stock. Reduce it over medium heat by one third and add the white wine. Measure 2 ¹/₄ cups (¹/₂ liter) and season to taste with salt, a little balsamic vinegar, Madeira, and truffle juice (the aspic must be rather strong in taste). Add the gelatin to enough cold water to soften for 3 to 4 minutes, then add this to the hot liquid and stir well to dissolve the gelatin, reheating if necessary. Strain through a fine sieve and let the aspic cool to room temperature until it is almost cold, but does not yet start to gel (if it has begun to gel, heat it a little before use).

Garnish:

Salt and pepper the chicken breast halves and sear them skin side down in the butter in a frying pan over medium heat, 4 to 5 minutes. Turn them and continue to cook 1 to 2 minutes longer. Remove the frying pan from the heat and let the breasts rest for a few minutes in the pan. Remove the skins. Sprinkle the breasts with a teaspoon of balsamic vinegar and add a teaspoon of minced tarragon. Let them cool completely.

Cut the breast halves lengthwise in ¹/₂ inch (1 cm) wide slices and flatten slightly with the side of a cleaver or heavy knife. Remove any yellow fat from the slices of foie gras and adapt the slices to the shape of the mold.

To assemble the terrine:

Oil the mold and line it with plastic wrap, being careful not to make creases. Mix ¹/₃ cup (80 ml) of aspic with the remaining tarragon and use it to coat the bottom of the mold. Cover with three slices of foie gras by arranging them side by side and let set with the aspic. Cover with a little more aspic and let set again. Soak half of the poultry sections at a time in a little liquid aspic and spread out flat over the aspic to make the second layer. Cover with a little aspic and put in the refrigerator. As soon as the aspic is set, start the assembly again with the remaining ingredients to obtain a terrine of 4 layers, finishing with a layer of aspic. Let the terrine rest in the refrigerator several hours or overnight.

To serve:

Detach the terrine from the mold by lifting the plastic wrap delicately and unmold it on a board. Cut it using an electric knife into slices of ¹/₂ inch (1 ¹/₂ cm) thickness. Serve the aspic sprinkled with coarsely ground pepper and sea salt, accompanied by slices of toasted farmhouse bread.

For additional garnishes you can serve cooked green beans, black truffle chopped in olive oil, and red beet syrup (p. 116).

COUNTRY-STYLE SALAD WITH RUSTIC VINAIGRETTE
SALADE PAYSANNE, VINAIGRETTE RUSTIQUE

Serves 4

Vinaigrette:
1 small shallot
¹/₂ small leek (white part only)
¹/₂ teaspoon Dijon mustard
fine sea salt
3 - 4 tablespoons white wine
vinegar
³/₄ cup (150 ml) neutral
vegetable oil (peanut or canola)
freshly ground black pepper

Salad:
2 extra fresh eggs
sea salt
7 ounces (200 g, 4 large handfuls)
mixed salad greens
2 homemade-type sandwich
or country-style bread slices
3 - 4 tablespoons (50 g)
clarified butter (p. 169)
6 thin slices skinned lean
and meaty salt pork

Vinaigrette:

Peel the shallot and finely mince. Wash and drain the leek and cut it crosswise into very fine strips. Whisk together the mustard, vinegar and a pinch of salt. Add the oil in a stream, while whisking, and whisk the dressing until it is emulsified. Correct the seasoning and pepper.

Salad:

Place the eggs in a pot of cold, salted water. Bring to the boil and cook them for 8 to 10 minutes, or until hard-boiled. Shock them in cold water, drain, and let cool. Peel the hard-boiled eggs and crush coarsely using a fork. Pick over the salad greens, tear into small pieces, wash and dry them. Remove the crust of the bread, cut the slices into small cubes, and fry with the clarified butter in a frying pan over medium heat until golden brown. Drain them on absorbent paper towels. Cut the slices of pork into small ¹/₄ inch (5 mm) sticks (lardons) in width and sauté them without additional fat in a hot frying pan until they become crispy. Drain these also.

Toss the salad greens with the vinaigrette and divide among four plates. Garnish the salads with the pork (lardons), croûtons and eggs, and serve.

Note:

The vinaigrette may be kept sealed in the refrigerator for two days.

ENDIVE SALAD WITH SCALLOPS AND ARTICHOKES
SALADE DE CHICONS AUX SAINT-JACQUES ET ARTICHAUTS

Serves 4

Salad:
4 - 6 small baby artichokes,
the number depending on their size
juice of half a lemon
3 small Belgian endives
8 ripe but firm cherry tomatoes
16 beautiful sea scallops
4 - 5 tablespoons olive oil
fine sea salt
freshly ground pepper

For Serving:
4 - 5 tablespoons elegant
vinaigrette (p. 168)
extra-virgin olive oil
balsamic vinegar reduction
(p. 170)
1 tablespoon fresh chives,
cut into sticks
a few sprigs of chervil

Salad:

Pare and trim the artichokes: i.e., remove the outer, hard leaves until more tender leaves appear. Cut the remaining leaves $^1/_2$ inch above the top of the artichoke base. Shorten the stems to $1^1/_2$ inches (4 cm). With a small knife, finely trim the artichokes top to bottom to obtain even artichoke bottoms. If necessary, continue trimming the circumference. Using a teaspoon or a melon baller, remove the choke from the center of the artichoke bottoms. Reserve the artichokes in water acidified with the lemon juice.

Wash the scallops under a thin stream of cold water, dry them and reserve them in the refrigerator. Separate the leaves of the Belgian endive and divide each leaf in half lengthwise. Wash and dry the tomatoes, and cut them into quarters.

Drain the artichoke bottoms, cut into very thin vertical slices and sauté them in 1 to 2 tablespoons of olive oil in a frying pan over high heat until they are quite crispy. Salt and pepper them and drain them on absorbent paper towels.

Heat the remaining olive oil in a large frying pan over medium heat. Salt and pepper the scallops and sear approximately 2 minutes per side to make them golden. Take the pan off the heat and put the scallops on a hot plate.

To serve:

Toss the leaves of Belgian endive and the tomatoes with the vinaigrette, and divide them among four plates. Arrange the artichoke slices and the scallops, drizzle with a little olive oil and reduced balsamic vinegar. Garnish with the sticks of chive and sprigs of chervil. Serve at once.

MARINATED FILLETS OF RED SNAPPER WITH EGGPLANT PURÉE

FILETS DE ROUGETS MARINÉS AU CAVIAR D'AUBERGINE

Serves 4

Eggplant purée:
2 small eggplants
4 shallots
fine sea salt
$^1/_4$ cup (50 - 60 ml)
extra-virgin olive oil
1 garlic clove

Marinade:
$^1/_2$ red bell pepper, peeled
8 pitted black olives
10 basil leaves
$^1/_4$ cup (60 ml) extra-virgin
olive oil
juice of half a lemon

Red snapper:
4 fillets red snapper 2 - 3 ounces
(60 to 70 g) each, boned but
with the skin
fine sea salt
freshly ground pepper
1 - 2 tablespoons olive oil

To serve:
fleur de sel or coarse sea salt
coarsely ground black pepper
balsamic vinegar

Eggplant purée:

Preheat the oven to 350°F (180°C).

Wash the eggplants, remove the ends, and halve. Peel and halve the shallots. Place the eggplants, cut side up, on a large piece of oiled heavy-duty aluminum foil and salt lightly. Add the shallots to the eggplants and drizzle a little bit of olive oil over all. Close up the foil and seal the edges tightly. Roast the eggplants for 50 minutes or until the flesh is very tender. Remove the package form the oven, open carefully, and let the contents cool.

Peel the garlic clove, halve lengthwise, remove the green germ, and blanch twice in boiling salted water. With a spoon, scrape the flesh out of the eggplants. Discard the seeds as well as the skins. Dry the eggplant pulp in a frying pan 5 minutes over low heat, stirring occasionally as needed. Then put the pulp, shallots, garlic and the remaining olive oil in a food processor bowl and process the whole to obtain a smooth paste. If the paste is too stiff, add a little more oil. Check the seasoning and reserve the eggplant purée at room temperature.

Marinade:

If you have not already done so, remove any remaining ribs and seeds from the sweet pepper half and cut the flesh into very small cubes. Cut the olives into thin slices. Wash the basil leaves, dry them and mince them finely. Combine together the sweet pepper cubes, the olives, the minced basil, the olive oil and a little lemon juice to taste.

Red snappers:

Rinse the fillets under a thin stream of cold water, dry them off and diagonally cut them in half. Heat a frying pan on medium heat, pour in the olive oil, distribute the fillets skin side down, and season. Let cook 2 to 3 minutes. Turn them over, and salt and pepper the other side. Take the frying pan from the heat and allow the fillets to continue to cook in the retained heat for another minute. Take them out and put them on a large soup plate or a dish. Pour the marinade over and let them marinate a few minutes, turning them over once.

To serve:

Place 2 tablespoons of eggplant purée in the center of each of four soup plates. Take the fillets out of the marinade, let them drain and place them skin side up on the eggplant purée. Sprinkle the skin with ground pepper and sea salt. Drizzle a band of marinade and a little balsamic vinegar around the red snapper fillets.

FIRST COURSES
ENTRÉES CHAUDES

EGGS "SURPRISE" WITH CAVIAR

ŒUFS SURPRISE AU CAVIAR

Serves 4

Vodka Cream:
3/5 cup (80 g) heavy cream
1 1/2 - 2 tablespoons (20 ml)
vodka
fine sea salt
a few drops fresh lemon juice

Eggs:
8 extra fresh eggs
fine sea salt
2 - 3 tablespoons
(30 - 40 g) butter
a pinch Cayenne pepper
1 ounce (35 g) salmon gravlax
or smoked salmon

For Serving:
4 teaspoons Sevruga caviar
(approximately 5 - 6 g per person)

Vodka Cream:
Whip the cream until it is quite stiff; add vodka, a little salt and a few drops lemon juice to taste. Put into an icing bag or pastry bag fitted with a small round tip. Reserve the cream in the refrigerator.

Eggs:
Open the eggs by slicing off the larger end with one neat cut using an egg cutter and empty them into a container. Rinse the four most perfect shells, dry them in a warm oven (125°F/50°C) and keep them warm until ready to use.

Cut the salmon into very small cubes and reserve them in the refrigerator. For scrambled eggs, prepare a water bath by heating water in a rather large saucepan. Put the eggs in a heatproof bowl and place that on the pan over the hot water. Start to swiftly beat the eggs with a whisk until they start to coagulate. Remove the bowl from the pan and immediately add the butter in small pieces, whisking constantly. Pass the eggs through a meshed sieve, and season them with the salt and Cayenne pepper.

To Serve:
Place the reserved shells, open end up, in eggcups. Fill initially with a teaspoon of salmon cubes, then fill the shells 3/4 of the way to the top with scrambled eggs, then, using an icing bag or pastry bag, pipe the vodka cream in two circles, one on top of the other, in order to obtain an edge on top of the egg shell. To finish, fill the "hole" with a good teaspoon of caviar and serve immediately.

Note:
In place of the shells, you can serve the eggs "surprise" in beautiful, heated eggcups.

BROILED OYSTERS WITH CUCUMBERS
HUÎTRES GRATINÉES AUX CONCOMBRES

Serves 4

Oysters:
1 small cucumber
1 tablespoon (15 g) butter
sea salt
24 beautiful oysters
approximately 2 - 4 pounds
(1 - 2 kg) coarse sea salt
or rock salt

Sabayon sauce:
4 egg yolks
1 scant cup (200 ml) dry
champagne or other sparkling wine
2 tablespoons (30 g) butter
fine sea salt
a few drops fresh lemon juice

Oysters:

Peel the cucumber and halve lengthwise. With a small spoon, remove the seeds. Chop the cucumber into very small cubes. Sauté the cubes in butter in a small frying pan over medium heat for 2 to 3 minutes until they are tender. Salt lightly and let cool on a kitchen towel.

Carefully open the oysters at the hinge. Reserve the oyster juice. Filter the oyster juice and pour it into a saucepan along with the oysters. Spread out the coarse salt in a large heat-resistant dish or on four large plates. Wash and dry the concave half of the oyster shells and arrange on the salt in such way that they're perfectly balanced.

Poach the oysters a few seconds in their juice, remove from the heat, and strain them, reserving their juice.

Sabayon sauce:

Measure $^1/_4$ cup (60 ml) of the oyster juice. Whisk the juice, the egg yolks and the champagne in a heatproof bowl. Place the bowl on a larger pot half filled with simmering water. Rapidly whisk the yolk mixture until you have a fine, pale yellow foam which has doubled in volume (sabayon). As soon as the mixture starts to thicken remove the bowl from the water bath and add the butter in small pieces, whisking constantly. Check the seasoning and add a few drops of lemon juice.

To Serve:

Turn on the broiler. In each shell, layer a teaspoon of cucumber and then a poached and drained oyster. Spoon 1 to 2 tablespoons of sabayon sauce onto each oyster. Broil the oysters, watching carefully and removing them as soon as they have turned golden. Serve six oysters per person on plates filled with coarse salt or directly from the larger serving dish.

Note:

You can use the clean coarse salt several times.

POTATO PANCAKES WITH SALMON GRAVLAX AND CAVIAR
GALETTES DE POMMES DE TERRE AU SAUMON MARINÉ ET CAVIAR

Serves 4

Gravlax:
Makes about 1 3/4 pounds (800 g)
(to be prepared at least 2 days
in advance)
2 cups (500 g) coarse sea salt
1 1/2 cups (350 g) sugar
1/2 cup (50 g) black pepper,
coarsely crushed
3/4 cup (80 g) dried fennel seeds
1 3/4 pounds (800 g) very fresh
wild salmon fillet with skin,
scaled and boned
(approximately half a salmon)

Cream:
3 tablespoons crème fraîche
or sour cream
2 tablespoons whipped cream
1 tablespoon heavy cream
fine sea salt
a few drops fresh lemon juice

Potato Pancakes:
1 3/4 pounds (800 g) of large
all-purpose potatoes (russet)
neutral vegetable oil for frying
fine sea salt
freshly ground pepper

For Serving:
6 teaspoons Sevruga caviar
(approximately 8 - 10 g per person)
8 sprigs of chives

Gravlax:

Combine the salt, sugar, pepper, and fennel seeds together in a small bowl. Spread a third of the mixture evenly in a deep dish the same size as the fish. Place the salmon in the dish, skin side down, and cover with the remaining salt mixture. Cover the dish with plastic wrap, place on the bottom shelf of the refrigerator and let sit for 36 to 48 hours (depending on the thickness of the flesh).

Take the salmon out of the dish, rinse thoroughly with cold water and then dry with absorbent paper towels. Slice the fillet diagonally into 12 very thin slices using a long, thin knife, such as a knife for slicing smoked salmon. Store any remaining salmon in the refrigerator for another use. Stack 3 salmon slices and cut with a 4-inch (10 cm) diameter pastry cutter. Do the same with the remaining slices to obtain 4 circles, each a stack of three thin slices. Store them covered in plastic wrap in the refrigerator.

Cream:

Stir the crème fraîche or sour cream with a whisk to loosen it, and then whisk it with the whipped cream and the heavy cream to obtain a semi-stiff cream. Season to taste with salt and lemon juice.

Potato Pancakes:

Peel the potatoes, wash them, and coarsely grate using a hand grater. Press out excess liquid between your hands, then salt and pepper the grated potatoes lightly. Put a tablespoon of oil in each of 4 small blini frying pans 4 inches (10 cm) in diameter, on rather high heat. Swirl the pans so that the oil completely coats the bottom. As soon as the oil is hot, fill each pan with grated potatoes to the edge without packing them too tightly, about 1/2 inch (1 cm) high. Let the pancakes brown uniformly on one side, lifting the edges once to spread out the oil. When they are well browned, turn them over, lower the heat and continue cooking until the blade of a knife inserted in the center goes in and comes out easily. Let the pancakes drain on absorbent paper towels and keep them warm in a preheated 125°F (50°C) oven.

Note:

If you do not have small frying pans, instead of separately making four small pancakes you can make one or two large ones, and then cut them into four circles using a pastry cutter.

To serve:

For each serving, place one three-layer stack of salmon on a hot potato pancake. Place on heated plates and garnish each one with a heaping tablespoonful of the cream and a heaping teaspoonful of caviar. Decorate with two sprigs of chives and serve at once.

CRISP PASTA PACKAGES STUFFED WITH RICOTTA
PÂTÉS CROUSTILLANTES FARCIES À LA RICOTTA

Serves 4

Stuffed pasta:
4 large leaves Swiss chard
(without the ribs)
1 small zucchini
2 tablespoons (25 g) butter
fine sea salt
1 bunch basil
12 ounces (350 g) ricotta cheese
2 eggs
2 ounces (60 g) freshly grated
Parmigiano-Reggiano cheese
freshly ground pepper
pinch of freshly grated nutmeg
10 ounces (250 g) homemade
pasta dough (p. 175)
4 tablespoons (50 g) melted
salted butter

Tomato sauce:
4 ripe but firm tomatoes
1 small onion
2 tablespoons olive oil
fine sea salt
freshly ground pepper
1 pinch of sugar
2 garlic cloves
1 fresh thyme sprig
2 - 3 tablespoons extra-virgin olive
oil

For Serving:
A little freshly grated
Parmigiano-Reggiano cheese

Stuffed pasta:

Remove the fine veins from the leaves of Swiss chard, wash and dry the leaves, and cut them into julienne. Trim off the ends of the zucchini, wash it and grate it coarsely. Sauté the two vegetables together with the butter in a frying pan, over low heat for 3 to 4 minutes. Salt slightly and let them cool. Pull the basil leaves from the stems, wash and dry them, and mince them. Mix well the ricotta, eggs, vegetables, the minced basil and the grated Parmigiano-Reggiano. Season the stuffing with salt, pepper and a pinch of nutmeg.

Roll out the pasta dough using a pasta machine or a rolling pin on a floured surface in order to obtain very fine bands of pasta 5 inches (12 cm) in width. Cut the bands into 5 x 5 inch (12 x 12 cm) squares and cook them for 1 to 2 minutes in plenty of salted, boiling water. Shock them in salted ice water and drain them well. Spread the pasta squares out on a dry kitchen towel. Place a tablespoon of the ricotta stuffing in the center of each square. To make the packages, fold three points over the top of the stuffing to cover it completely and fold the fourth remaining point underneath the small package. Place the pasta packages tightly against one another in a buttered gratin dish and, using a pastry brush, paint them uniformly with the melted salted butter.

Tomato sauce:

Remove the cores of the tomatoes and plunge them into boiling water for about 20 seconds. Shock them in cold water and remove the skins and seeds. Place the tomatoes in the bowl of an electric mixer or a food processor and purée them. Pass the purée through a fine-meshed sieve. Peel the onion, chop into small dice, and sauté for a few minutes until translucent in a pan with the olive oil. Add the tomato purée, season with salt, pepper and a pinch of sugar. Peel the garlic cloves, slice in half, and remove the green germ. Add the garlic halves and the thyme sprig to the tomato sauce. Cook the sauce for 15 to 20 minutes over low heat until it starts to thicken. Remove the garlic and thyme, add the extra-virgin olive oil and check the seasoning.

To Serve:

Preheat the oven to 400°F (200°C). Put the dish in the hot oven and cook the packages 5 to 8 minutes so that they become golden brown and crisp. Serve 2 to 3 pasta packages per person on heated plates and accompany with the tomato sauce and grated Parmigiano-Reggiano cheese.

CREAMY RISOTTO WITH WILD MUSHROOMS
RISOTTO CRÉMEUX AUX CHAMPIGNONS DES BOIS

Serves 4

Risotto:
1 shallot
4 tablespoons olive oil
1 ¹/₂ cups (300 g) Italian
superfino rice (Arborio)
fine sea salt
¹/₂ cup (100 ml) dry sparkling
wine or white wine
Approximately 1 quart (liter)
hot chicken stock (p. 172)

For serving:
6 ounces (150 g) of mixed,
wild mushrooms (porcini,
chanterelles, trompettes des
Morts etc., or other strong
flavored mushrooms)
4 tablespoons (60 g) butter
fine sea salt
freshly ground pepper
2 ounces (60 g) freshly grated
Parmigiano-Reggiano cheese
4 tablespoons whipped cream
extra-virgin olive oil
4 leaves of fried flat-leaf parsley
(p. 170)

Risotto:

Peel the shallot, finely mince, and sauté briefly in the olive oil in a large cast iron casserole. Add the unwashed rice. Sauté over low heat until it becomes translucent. Moisten with the wine and let it evaporate completely. Add a ladleful of hot chicken stock. As soon as the rice has absorbed the liquid, continue adding the rest of the stock by ladlefuls, stirring frequently. Wait until each has been absorbed before adding the next. Continue to stir with a wooden spoon until the rice is just cooked, but not yet completely tender (al dente).

For serving:

While the rice is cooking, clean the mushrooms without washing them. Cut them according to their size into halves or quarters. Place a frying pan on medium heat and when the pan is quite hot add two teaspoons of the butter and sauté the mushrooms. Season them with salt and pepper and keep them in a warm spot or on very low heat. When the rice is done, remove the casserole from the heat, stir in the remaining butter in small pieces and the grated Parmigiano-Reggiano cheese. Finally, incorporate the whipped cream. Check the seasoning and divide the risotto among four heated soup plates. Garnish with the sautéed wild mushrooms, drizzle with the extra-virgin olive oil, top with the fried parsley, and serve at once.

GREEN RISOTTO WITH CRISPY BACON
RISOTTO VERT AU LARD CROUSTILLANT

Serves 4

Bacon:
8 very thin slices of salted pork
(in this case, choose streak o' lean
or unsmoked bacon)

Risotto:
1 shallot
4 tablespoons olive oil
1 1/2 cups (300 g) Italian
superfino rice (Arborio)
fine sea salt
1/2 cup (100 ml) dry sparkling
or white wine
Approximately 1 quart (liter)
hot chicken stock (p. 172)
1 head of Boston, Butter,
or Green Leaf lettuce
(look for lettuce with fresh,
very green leaves)
2 tablespoons (30 g) butter
2 ounces (60 g) freshly grated
Parmigiano-Reggiano cheese
3 tablespoons whipped cream

Garnish:
a small piece (1 - 2 tablespoons)
Parmigiano-Reggiano to shave
for garnish
4 leaves of fried flat-leaf parsley
(p. 170)

Bacon:

Preheat the oven to 325°F (160°C). Place the sections of pork side by side on a baking sheet lined with parchment paper. Cover the slices with a second sheet slightly smaller than the first in order to flatten them well. Cook them in the hot oven for 15 to 20 minutes until the bacon has rendered its fat and is quite crisp. Take them out of the oven, remove the top sheet, and drain the bacon between sheets of absorbent paper toweling.

Risotto:

Peel the shallot, finely mince, and sauté briefly in the olive oil in a large cast iron casserole. Add the unwashed rice. Sauté over low heat until it becomes translucent. Moisten with the wine and let it evaporate completely. Add a ladleful of hot chicken stock. As soon as the rice has absorbed the liquid, continue adding the rest of the broth by ladlefuls, stirring frequently. Wait until each has been absorbed before adding the next. Continue to stir with a wooden spoon until the rice is just cooked, but not yet completely tender (al dente).

Clean the lettuce and select the greenest leaves. Remove the ribs from the green leaves and wash the leaves. Drain them and then blanch them for 1 minute in plenty of salted boiling water. Shock them in ice water, drain them and press them well between your hands. Put them in the bowl of an electric mixer or a food processor and mix them to a fine purée.

As soon as the rice is finished cooking, remove the casserole from the heat, stir in the butter in small pieces and add as much of the lettuce purée as needed until the risotto has a beautiful green color. Finally, add in the Parmigiano-Reggiano and incorporate the whipped cream. Check the seasoning. Divide the risotto between heated soup plates. Garnish each plate with two crispy slices of bacon, some shavings of Parmigiano-Reggiano and a fried parsley leaf. Serve immediately.

WILD MUSHROOMS IN PUFF PASTRY
CHAUSSONS AUX CHAMPIGNONS DES BOIS

Serves 4

Stuffing:
10 ounces (250 g) small,
white, cultivated mushrooms
1 shallot
3 tablespoons (50 g) butter
fine sea salt
freshly ground pepper
a few drops of fresh lemon juice
10 ounces (250 g)
mixed wild mushrooms
(for example: porcini, chanterelles,
morels, etc., or other strong
flavored mushrooms)

Completion:
1/2 pound (200 g) puff pastry
(p. 175)
1 egg yolk

Stuffing:

Prepare the cultivated mushrooms by cutting off the sandy feet, wiping clean with a damp towel, and finely chopping. Peel the shallot, chop fine and sauté just until soft in a frying pan in 2 tablespoons (30 g) of butter. Add the mushrooms, salt, pepper and a few drops of lemon juice. Sauté the mixture for 5 to 8 minutes on medium heat until the excess water evaporates and the mixture is homogenous and fairly dry. Let the mixture cool on a plate.

Clean the wild mushrooms carefully, wash if necessary (morels) and cut them, depending on their size, in slices or halves and quarters. Sauté the mushrooms in a well-heated frying pan in the remaining butter. Salt them and let cool.

Completion:

Preheat the oven to 400°F (200°C).

Roll out the puff pastry to $1/8$ inch (3 mm) thickness and cut it using a pastry cutter into 8 circles 4 inches (10 cm) in diameter. Whisk the egg yolk with 1 tablespoon of water. Lightly paint the edges of four circles with the egg wash using a pastry brush. Place in the center of each circle, two tablespoons of the cultivated mushroom mixture. Divide the sautéed wild mushrooms among the four pastries and cover them with the remaining circles to obtain small packages. Press the edges well between your fingers in order to seal them. Make a small hole with a point of knife in the top of each package so that the cooking steam can escape.

Place the packages on a baking sheet lined with parchment paper and paint evenly with the remaining egg wash. Cook for 10 minutes in a pre-heated oven at 400°F (200°C) and then lower the temperature to 350°F (180°C) and continue cooking 15 minutes until the packages are well browned. Take them out of the oven and let cool a little before tasting them. Serve accompanied by a small mixed salad.

"KNIDDELEN" - LUXEMBOURG-STYLE FLOUR DUMPLINGS
QUENELLES DE FARINE À LA LUXEMBOURGEOISES

Serves 3 to 4

Dumplings:
*3 slices homemade-type sandwich
bread*
$^1/_2$ cup (150 ml) milk
*1 pound (500 g, 3 $^1/_2$ - 4 cups)
sifted flour*
5 - 6 eggs
fine sea salt
2 tablespoons (30 g) melted butter

Sauce:
*2 slices homemade-type sandwich
bread*
*2 tablespoons (30 g)
clarified butter (p. 169)*
*6 - 7 thin slices (100 g) salt pork
(choose streak o' lean
or unsmoked bacon)*
$^1/_3$ cup (120 g) heavy cream
fine sea salt

For serving:
2 tablespoons minced fresh chives

Dumplings:

Remove the crusts of the bread, then tear it into small pieces and soak them in milk. Place the flour in a bowl, add the eggs, salt, the bread and milk, and combine the whole by firmly beating with a wooden spoon, until it becomes a smooth and semi-firm batter. Then incorporate the melted butter. Set the batter aside covered with plastic wrap for half an hour.

Fill a large pot with water, bring to the boil and add salt. Using a tablespoon, form small dumplings of batter and poach them for 3 to 4 minutes in the simmering water. Avoid putting too many dumplings in at the same time, so that they can cook evenly. Remove the dumplings with a skimmer and drain well in a strainer or colander. Arrange in a heated gratin dish and keep warm.

Sauce:

Remove the crusts and the cut the bread slices into small cubes. Prepare the croûtons as described on p. 24.

Slice the pork into thin sticks (lardons) and sauté them in a hot frying pan until they are quite crisp. Degrease the frying pan by removing the pork and wiping the inside with paper toweling. Add the cream to the pan and heat. Check the seasoning. Return the lardons to the sauce.

To serve:

Coat the Kniddelen with the sauce and bacon. Sprinkle with croûtons and minced chives. Serve piping hot.

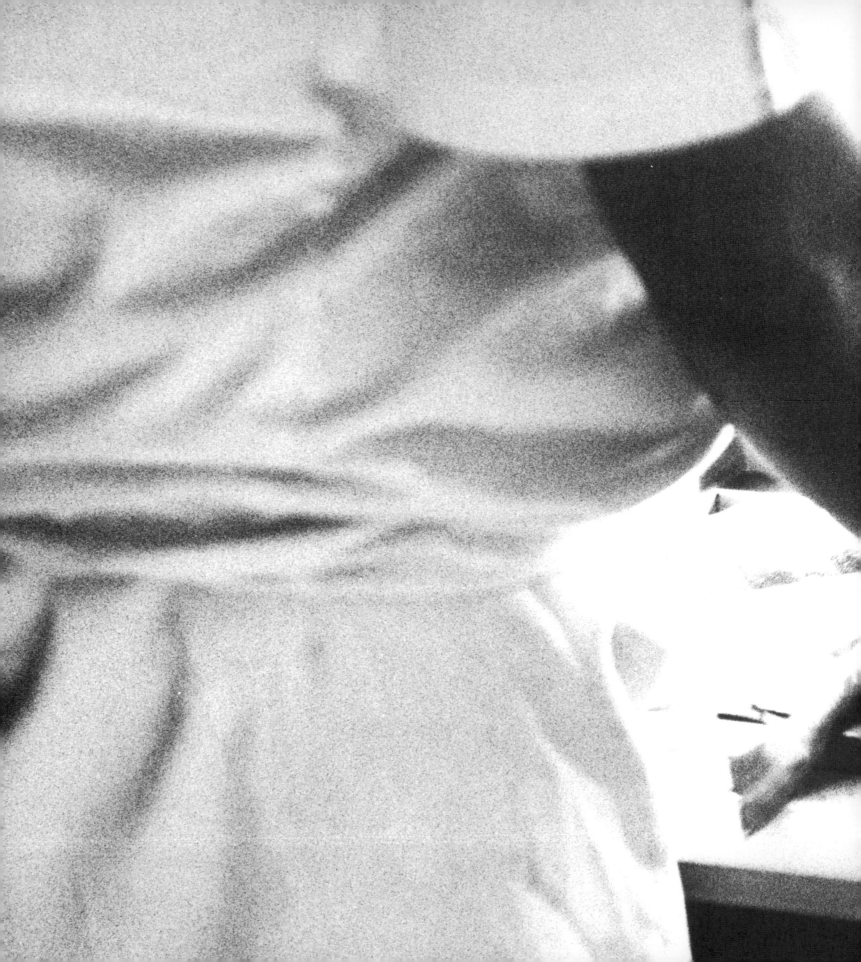

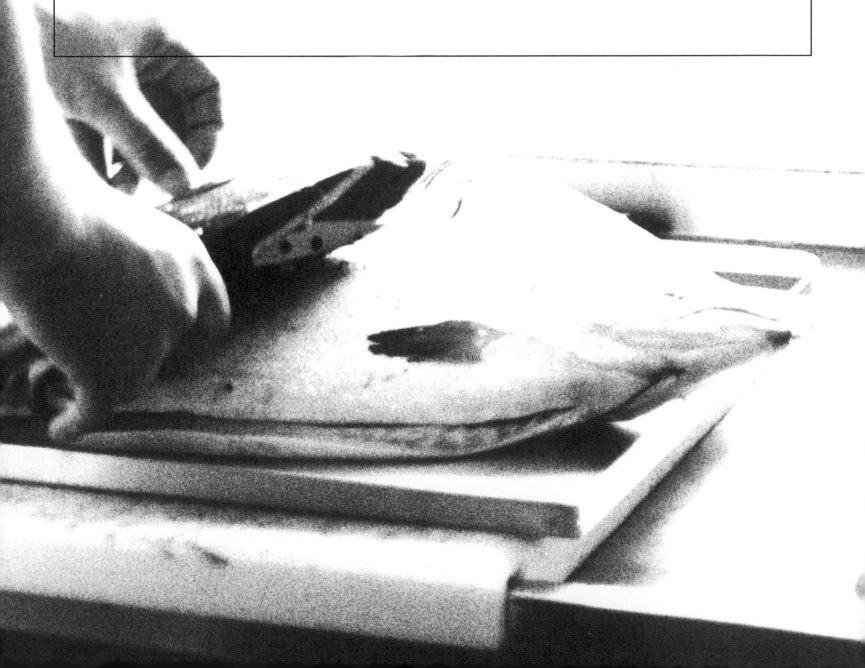

FISH AND SHELLFISH
POISSONS, CRUSTACÉS ET COQUILLAGES

MUSSELS IN SAFFRON SAUCE
RAGOÛT DE MOULES AU SAFRAN

Serves 4

Mussels:
4 pounds (2 kg) mussels
1 small leek
(white and pale green part only)
1 shallot
1 celery stalk
1 medium carrot
fine sea salt
1 1/2 tablespoons (20 g) butter
1 tablespoon olive oil
1 cup (1/4 liter) dry white wine
1 fresh thyme sprig

Sauce:
1 teaspoon mild curry
6 saffron filaments
1/2 cup (100 g) heavy cream
2 tablespoons (30 g) cold butter
fine sea salt
freshly ground pepper

To serve:
1 tablespoon olive oil
2 tablespoons finely minced
fresh chives

Mussels:

Carefully wash the mussels in very cold or ice water, scrape them well and trim off the beards. Discard any half-opened mussels.

Clean the leek, halve lengthwise, wash and dry it, and then cut it in very small dice. Peel the shallot and mince finely. Peel the celery stalk and carrot. Initially slice lengthwise into thin (1/4 inch, 1/2 cm) slices with the aid of a mandoline (Benriner), then in sticks lengthwise and then in very small cubes (brunoise). Blanch a heaping tablespoon of each vegetable in salted boiling water, shock in ice water and drain. Reserve.

Sauté the remaining vegetable cubes for a few minutes in butter in a pot large enough for the mussels, on medium heat, until they are quite tender. Add the white wine and the thyme and let simmer 3 to 4 minutes. Add the mussels, cover, and cook for 4 to 5 minutes. Stir up once or twice during the course of cooking. As soon as the shells open, take the mussels out with a skimmer, and discard any that are unopened. Pass the cooking broth through a fine sieve into a small saucepan. Shell the mussels, cover with plastic wrap and reserve.

Sauce:

Reduce the cooking broth by a third. Add the curry and the saffron and let simmer over low heat for a few minutes. Pour in the cream and mix the sauce with an immersion blender or hand mixer, adding the butter in small pieces. Season with salt and pepper.

To serve:

Heat the blanched vegetable cubes in a frying pan with oil on low heat. Add the mussels. Heat and distribute the mussels and vegetable mixture into four hot soup plates. Remix the sauce to make it foam and coat the mussels with it. Sprinkle with the chives and serve.

SCALLOPS IN SEALED SHELLS
SAINT-JACQUES EN COQUILLES LUTÉE

Serves 4

Scallops:
4 small porcini
$^1/_4$ pound (100 g)
trompettes des morts/horns
of plenty mushrooms
(or other strong flavored
mushrooms)
1 shallot
1 - 2 tablespoons (20 g) butter
fine sea salt
8 - 12 sea scallops
(depending on their size), cleaned
4 well shaped scallop shells (with
lid, or 8 shells matched for size)
$^1/_4$ pound (100 g) puff pastry
(p. 174)
1 egg yolk

Sauce:
1 shallot
3 tablespoons (50 g) butter
$^1/_4$ teaspoon (1 knife point)
finely minced garlic
trimmings of mushrooms
1 cup (200 ml) chicken stock
(p. 172)
$^1/_3$ cup (80 ml) full-fat milk
$^1/_3$ cup (80 g) heavy cream
fine sea salt
freshly ground pepper
1 - 2 tablespoons (20 ml) dry
sherry (Tio Pepe)

To serve:
coarse sea salt or rock salt
(optional)

Scallops:

Clean the porcini with a damp towel, peel and slice them in to regularly shaped slices. Clean the trompettes des morts wash and dry them, and halve or quarter them. Reserve the trimmings. Peel the shallot and mince finely. Sauté the mushrooms in a hot frying pan with the butter until they are lightly browned and cooked through, 4 to 5 minutes or so, add the minced shallot and salt lightly. Let cool.

Wash the scallops under a stream of cold water, dry them with absorbent paper towels and reserve in the refrigerator. Clean the shells well inside and outside with a brush. Wash and dry them.

Roll out the puff pastry to $^1/_8$ inch (3 mm) and cut out four strips long enough to completely encircle the scallop shells and $1^1/_4$ inch (3 cm) width. Mix the egg yolk with a tablespoon of water. Preheat the oven to 400°F (200°C). Salt the scallops and place 2 to 3 scallops in each of four hollow shells. Distribute the mushrooms around and close with the shell lids (or with another matching shells). Glaze the pastry rings on one side with the egg yolk. Cover the opening between the halves of shells with the glazed side. Press the pastry well against the sides of the shells to seal them, then glaze.

Cook the shells in the preheated oven 14 to 15 minutes, until the puff pastry has a beautiful golden color.

Sauce:

While the scallops are cooking, peel the shallot, slice it and sauté it in a small pan in 1 tablespoon (15 g) of butter. Add the garlic and the mushroom trimmings. Allow to cook slowly for a few minutes, add the chicken stock. Let reduce by half, then pass through a fine sieve. Pour in the milk and the cream. Whisk while adding the remaining butter in small pieces. Season the sauce, and scent it with the sherry to taste.

To serve:

Check the seasoning of the sauce and mix with an immersion blender to make it foam. Spread out good handful of coarse salt in the center of four soup plates. Take the cooked shells and place them on the salt. Serve still closed and accompanied by the sauce.

RAVIOLI WITH LANGOUSTINE FILLING
RAVIOLI AUX LANGOUSTINES

Serves 4

Ravioli:
12 large fresh langoustines or large
fresh shrimp
6 1/2 ounces (200 g) fresh pasta
dough (p. 175)
flour for the work surface
1 egg white, slightly beaten
sea salt

Sauce:
1 ripe but firm tomato
3/4 cup (200 ml) shrimp stock
(p. 171)
6 saffron filaments
3 tablespoons (50 g) cold butter
fine sea salt
2 tablespoons whipped cream

Garnish:
1 1/2 - 1 3/4 pounds (700 g)
baby spinach
2 tablespoons (30 g) butter
fine sea salt
freshly ground pepper
a few sprigs of chervil

Ravioli:

Remove the heads of the crayfish or shrimp and peel the tails. Divide the tails in half, tear of the vein and slice into 3/4 inch (2 cm) pieces. Reserve covered with plastic wrap in the refrigerator.

Flour your work surface. Spread out the pasta dough using a pasta machine or a rolling pin into long very thin bands. Lightly glaze half of the bands with the beaten egg white. Salt the flesh of the crayfish/shrimp and place 24 portions (of approximately a teaspoon) in the center of the glazed bands, spacing them 3 inches (8 cm) apart. Cover as smoothly as possible with the remaining bands, while trying to avoid creasing the pasta. Delicately press the band higher around the stuffing. Cut out the ravioli with a 3 inch (8 cm) diameter circular pastry cutter. Seal and flatten the edges well using your fingers. Reserve the ravioli on a floured plate.

Sauce:

Remove the core of the tomato, plunge for 20 seconds in boiling water, shock, remove the skin, quarter and remove the seeds. Cut the tomato quarters in 1/4 inch (5 mm) dice. Reduce the shrimp stock by half, add the saffron filaments and let them infuse for a moment. Blend the sauce with an immersion blender or hand mixer, adding the butter in small pieces. Salt.

Garnish:

Pick through the spinach leaves, wash and dry well. Right before serving, sauté them for 2 minutes in a hot frying pan in the butter. Salt and pepper. Let drain on absorbent paper towels and keep warm.

To serve:

Poach the ravioli 2 to 3 minutes in simmering salted water. Remove with a skimmer and drain them on a kitchen towel.

Place portions of the spinach in the center of four heated plates. Place 6 ravioli on each plate. Mix the sauce to make it foam, add the diced tomatoes and the whipped cream, and check the seasoning. Coat the ravioli with the sauce, garnish with the chervil sprigs and serve at once.

HALF LOBSTER WITH HERBS
DEMI-HOMARD AUX HERBES

Serves 4

Herb butter:

*8 tablespoons (120 g) butter
at room temperature
1 tablespoon finely minced
tarragon leaves
1 - 2 tablespoons coarsely
chopped parsley
1 tablespoon finely minced
watercress leaves
fine sea salt
freshly ground pepper
1 - 2 tablespoons (20 ml) pastis
(anis liquor)
a few drops fresh lemon juice*

Lobsters:

*around 6 quarts/liters
court-bouillon for lobster (p. 172)
2 large lobsters, 1 1/4 - 1 1/2
pounds (600 - 700 g) each*

Herb butter:

Combine the softened butter well with the herbs and season with salt, pepper, pastis and a few drops of lemon juice. Reserve in the refrigerator until needed.

Lobsters:

Bring the court-bouillon to a boil. Plunge in a lobster and cook it for 3 minutes. Take it out of the court-bouillon and let it rest at least 3 minutes before splitting it and shelling. Cook the second lobster in the same way.

Remove the claws and the tails of lobsters. Using the back of a large knife or a lobster shell cracker (grip), delicately break the claws and the divisions of the "arms", then shell them. Divide the lobsters (tails and heads) in half lengthwise. Discard the sand sack and vein, and empty the heads carefully. Cut the shelled lobster flesh (claws and divisions) into pieces and fill in the heads.

Completion:

Preheat the oven to 350°F (180°C).

Dot the lobster halves with flakes of the herb butter. Place the lobsters side by side on a heat-proof plate or a large gratin dish. Finish the cooking for 6 to 8 minutes in the preheated oven until the flesh is quite hot and the butter melted. Serve the broiled half lobsters on heated plates accompanied by white country-style bread or baguette.

CRISP PASTA "ROSES" WITH LOBSTER
NOUILLES CROUSTILLANTES DE HOMARD

Serves 4

Pasta "roses":
around 6 quarts/liters
court-bouillon for lobster (p. 172)
2 lobsters, 1 1/4 pound
(600 g) each
1 carrot
1/4 pound (120 g)
celery root (celeriac)
1 1/2 tablespoons (20 g) butter
fine sea salt
6 1/2 ounces (200 g)
fresh pasta dough (p. 175)
flour for the work surface

Completion:
3 1/2 tablespoons (50 g)
melted salted butter
1 tablespoon olive oil
fine sea salt
Spice sauce (p. 90, the same as
for the pike soufflés)

Crisp "roses":

Bring the court-bouillon to a boil. Plunge in a lobster and cook it for 5 minutes at the simmer. Take it out of the court-bouillon and let it cool before shelling it. Cook the second lobster in the same way. Remove the claws and the tails of lobsters. Using the back of a large knife or a lobster shell cracker (grip), delicately break the claws and the divisions of the "arms" without damaging the flesh of the claws, and shell them. Divide the lobster tails in half lengthwise. Discard the vein and take the flesh out of the shells. Cut the shelled lobster flesh (except the claws) into 3/4 inch (2 cm) slices. Reserve covered with plastic wrap.

Peel the carrot and celery root and slice, initially using a mandoline (Benrinder), into fine lengthwise slices. Cut the slices into matchsticks, then into very small cubes. Sauté the cubes a few minutes in a small pan in butter and a tablespoon of water. Season with salt.

Lightly flour your work surface. Quarter the pasta dough. Roll out the portions of dough using a pasta machine or with a rolling pin into four very fine bands (approximately 6 inches wide by 14 inches long / 15 cm x 35 cm). To make very thin bands, pass twice through the pasta machine set at its finest setting. Cook them 1 to 2 minutes in simmering salted water. Shock in cold salted water, and then place them on a towel, drying both sides off.

Completion:

Preheat the oven to 425°F (220°C). Toss the lobster meat with the vegetable cubes. Spread out a quarter of the mixture on the lower third of each band, lengthwise. Roll up the bands starting with the stuffed edge, leaving a free edge of 3/4 inches (2 cm) at the top. Then, starting on one end, roll the rolls in the shape of a rose or snail. Place them, free edge up, in a buttered gratin dish, spacing them a little apart. Glaze each rose, especially the edges, with the melted salted butter. Cook them for 6 minutes in the preheated oven until the pasta is golden and crisp.

While the roses are in the oven, heat the claws in a frying pan on low heat in the olive oil and salt lightly. To serve, take the roses from the gratin dish with an offset spatula and place them in hot soup plates. Garnish with a claw and serve accompanied by spice sauce (p. 90).

WILD SALMON WITH POTATOES AND BASIL BUTTER

PAVÉS DE SAUMON SAUVAGE AU BEURRE DE BASILIC

Serves 4

Garnish:
16 small waxy potatoes
(for example: Yukon Gold)
fine sea salt
2 tablespoons (30 g) butter
freshly ground pepper

Salmon:
4 thick slices of wild salmon fillets
without skin and bones,
4 1/2 ounces (140 g) each
fine sea salt
freshly ground pepper
2 tablespoons olive oil

Basil Butter:
1 shallot
juice of half a lemon
5 tablespoons (70 - 80 g)
cold butter
fine sea salt
10 large basil leaves

To serve:
a few sprigs of chervil

Garnish:
Wash the potatoes and cook them in boiling, salted water approximately 25 minutes until they are tender. Drain and let them cool. Halve lengthwise and brown them in butter in a hot frying pan. Season and keep warm.

Salmon:
Slightly trim the edges of the fillets slices to obtain thick square pieces. Salt and pepper the fillets on both sides. Sear for 3 minutes in a frying pan over medium heat, skin side first. Turn them over and continue cooking for 1 to 2 minutes. Remove the frying pan from the heat and leave the fillets to rest.

Basil Butter:
Peel the shallot, mince finely and cook it in a small pan in $1/2$ cup (100 ml) of water, until the water is reduced by half. Add the lemon juice and thicken the sauce with butter: incorporate the cold butter in small pieces by swirling the pan by its handle, obtaining a smooth and shiny emulsion (do not let it boil). Salt. Wash and dry the basil leaves and slice into a fine julienne. Add to the sauce.

To serve:
Distribute the salmon squares and the potatoes on four hot plates, pour a ribbon of basil butter around the salmon and coat the potatoes. Garnish with chervil sprigs and serve at once.

SOLE FILLETS WITH CRAYFISH AND FRESH PASTA
FILETS DE SOLES, ÉCREVISSES ET PÂTES FRAÎCHES

Serves 4

Pasta:
6 ¹/₂ ounces (200 g) fresh pasta
dough (p. 175)
flour for the work surface
2 small tender leeks

Langoustines:
3 quarts/liters court-bouillon
for lobster (p. 172)
12 live crayfish (to be ordered
from your fishmonger)

Sole:
8 fillets of Dover sole 2 - 2 ¹/₄
ounces (60 - 70 g) each
fine sea salt
1 - 2 tablespoons (20 g) butter
¹/₃ cup (80 ml) dry champagne
or sparkling wine
2 - 3 tablespoons (40 ml)
dry Sherry (Tio Pepe)
¹/₂ cup (100 ml)
chicken stock (p. 172)
2 - 2 ¹/₂ tablespoons (30 - 40 g)
cold butter

To serve:
2 tablespoons (30 g) butter
fine sea salt
2 tablespoons finely minced chives

Pasta:

Lightly flour your work surface. Roll out the dough using a pasta machine in 1 inch (2 - 3 mm) thin bands. Cut the bands in pieces 10 - 12 inches (25 - 30 cm) long and then into spaghetti or tagliatelle. Place them on a floured plate, without piling them up, until use.

Clean the leeks, remove the dark green part, halve lengthwise, and wash and dry them. Cut the halves into 1 ¹/₂ - 2 inch (4 - 5 cm) pieces and then into fine julienne.

Crayfish:

Bring the court-bouillon to a boil. Plunge in the crayfish and cook for 2 to 3 minutes at a simmer. Remove them with a skimmer and shock with salted cold water. Remove the heads of the crayfish, peel the tails and the claws, and de-vein the tails. Reserve the crayfish flesh under plastic wrap.

Sole:

Delicately flatten the fillets of sole between two sheets of plastic wrap. Season with salt and pepper. Sauté them lightly for 3 to 4 minutes, on both sides, in 1 ¹/₂ tablespoons of butter in a large hot sauté pan over medium heat, without letting them color. Take them out of the sauté pan and keep them warm on a hot plate.

Deglaze the sauté pan with champagne, let it reduce to a syrup, add the sherry and chicken stock. Let the sauce simmer for a moment and thicken it with the butter: add the cold butter in small pieces by giving a light rotational movement to the sauté pan to thicken the sauce. Season with salt.

To serve:

While the fillets are cooking, cook the pasta and the julienne of leeks together in salted boiling water. Drain, reserving a little of the cooking water. Put the pasta in a large frying pan, add a few tablespoons of the cooking water and 1 ¹/₂ tablespoons (20 g) of butter. Toss lightly together over very low heat. Salt lightly.

Reheat the crayfish in a small frying pan in the remaining butter over low heat and season. Add the chives to the sauce. Take a quarter of the pasta-leek mixture, using a meat fork, and arrange lengthwise in the center of a heated plate. Cover the pasta with two fillets and coat with the chive sauce. Dress the three remaining plates in the same way. Garnish each plate with three crayfish tails and claws. Serve at once.

HALIBUT STEAKS IN CASSEROLE WITH CHANTERELLES

CÔTES DE TURBOT EN COCOTTE AUX GIROLLES

Serves 2

Jacqueline's stock:
1 carrot
1 onion
$^1/_2$ bulb of fennel
1 leek (white part only)
2 celery stalks
$1^1/_2$ tablespoons (20 g) of butter
$^1/_2$ cup (0.125 liter)
dry champagne or sparkling wine
6 cups ($1^1/_2$ liter) chicken stock
1 fresh thyme sprig
1 garlic clove

Garnish:
6 very small round potatoes
sea salt
2 tablespoons olive oil

Halibut:
1 shallot
$6 - 6^1/_2$ ounces (200 g) small
chanterelle mushrooms
2 halibut steaks with bone $1^1/_4$ -
$1^1/_2$ inches (3 - 4 cm) thick,
10 ounces (300 g) each
fine sea salt
freshly ground pepper
3 - 4 tablespoons olive oil
1 garlic clove
$^1/_2$ cup (0.125 liter)
dry champagne or sparkling wine
$^1/_2$ cup (100 ml) fish stock
(p. 171)
1 cup ($^1/_4$ liter) Jacqueline's stock
2 - 3 tablespoons (40 ml) dry
Sherry (Tio Pepe)
2 tablespoons coarsely chopped
parsley

To serve:
fleur de sel or coarse sea salt
coarsely ground black pepper

Jacqueline's broth:
Clean the vegetables, peel and wash them, and thinly slice. Sauté 4 to 5 minutes in the butter in a saucepan. Deglaze with the champagne, let reduce to a syrup and add the chicken stock. Add the thyme and the garlic clove and let the stock simmer approximately 2 hours on low heat. Pass it through a sieve, pressing well to extract the juices, and then let reduce to a third. Reserve in the refrigerator until needed (the stock can be prepared 3 days in advance).

Garnish:
Wash the potatoes and steam them in their skins until they are tender. Let them cool and flatten them to $^1/_2$ inch (1 cm) thickness with the flat side of a large knife to make them burst. When ready to serve, brown the potatoes on both sides in olive oil in a frying pan over medium heat.

Halibut:
Peel and mince the shallot. Clean the chanterelles with a moist paper towel and either halve or quarter them, depending on their size.

Salt and pepper the halibut steaks and sear on both sides in 2 tablespoons of olive oil in a large cast iron casserole. Add the garlic clove during the cooking. Take the steaks out of the casserole and degrease. Deglaze the coagulated juices in the casserole with the champagne, let reduce to a syrup, add the fish stock and let reduce again. Add Jacqueline's stock and the halibut steaks. Braise the steaks, covered, for 10 minutes over low heat.

While the halibut is cooking, sauté the chanterelles for 1 to 2 minutes in the remaining olive oil in a hot frying pan on medium heat. Add the shallot and salt lightly. Remove the lid of the casserole, add the chanterelles and cook 5 minutes longer. Season the cooking juices with salt and pepper. Scent it with sherry and strew with parsley.

To serve:
Arrange the halibut steaks and chanterelles on two heated plates, coat with a little of the cooking juices. Place 3 potatoes per person beside the steaks. Sprinkle with coarsely ground pepper and fleur de sel. Garnish the plates with chervil sprigs and serve the halibut accompanied by the remaining cooking juices in a sauceboat.

SEA BASS IN A SALT CRUST, FENNEL SAUCE

LOUP DE MER EN CROÛTE DE SEL, SAUCE FENOUIL

Serves 2

Sea bass:

*1 medium size whole sea bass,
scaled, 1 1/4 - 1 1/2 pounds
(600 - 700 g)
4 fresh thyme sprigs
3 - 4 pounds (1 1/2 - 2 kg) coarse
sea salt (depending on the size
of the fish)*

Sauce:

*makes about 1 1/2 - 2 cups
(300 - 400 ml), serves 3 to 4
1 fennel bulb
2 shallots
2 1/2 tablespoons (40 g) butter
1 fresh thyme sprig
a few dried fennel seeds
1/2 cup (100 ml) dry white wine
2 - 3 tablespoons (40 ml) Noilly
Prat or other dry white vermouth
1 3/4 cups (400 ml)
fish stock (p. 171)
1/2 cup (100 g) heavy cream
1/2 cup (100 ml) milk
fine sea salt
freshly ground pepper
a few drops fresh lemon juice*

Sea Bass:

Preheat the oven to 400°F (200°C). Remove the gills of the fish, rinse under a stream of cold water, dry well between absorbent paper towels, and line the belly with the thyme sprigs.

Mix the sea salt with approximately 3/4 - 1 cup (200 ml) of cold water until it is just wet. Spread out a quarter of the salt to a depth of 1/2 inch (1 cm) over a baking sheet or roaster lined with parchment paper that is large enough to hold the fish. Place the fish on the salt and cover entirely with the remaining salt.

Cook the sea bass for 15 to 20 minutes in the preheated oven to an internal temperature of 125 - 130°F (55 - 60°C). To check the temperature, you can insert an instant reading thermometer into the fish after 15 minutes of cooking. Take the fish from the oven and let it rest for 5 minutes before breaking the salt crust with a hammer or the back of a large kitchen knife. Delicately remove the fish from the salt crust and place it on a large heated platter.

Sauce:

Clean the fennel, quarter, then chop it up. Peel the shallot and mince. Cook the fennel and shallot in half (20 g) of the butter over low heat in a small pan without allowing them to color. Deglaze with the white wine and Noilly Prat (vermouth), and let reduce to a syrup. Add the fish stock, thyme, and a few fennel seeds. Reduce to half. Pour in the milk and the cream, and let simmer for 5 more minutes. Pass the sauce through a fine sieve and blend with an immersion blender or hand mixer, adding the remaining butter in small pieces. Season with salt and pepper and a few drops of lemon juice to taste.

To serve:

To release the fillets, remove the top skin of the fish. Delicately detach the first fillet from the backbone (fish frame) and place it on the hot platter. Remove the backbone using a fork, starting with the tail. While lifting the backbone, hold down the second fillet using a spoon. Place the second fillet on the platter. Serve the fillets accompanied by the fennel sauce in a sauceboat and a little extra-virgin olive oil.

GRATINÉED SOUFFLÉS OF PIKE, SPICE SAUCE
SOUFFLÉS DE BROCHET GRATINÉS, SAUCE AUX ÉPICES

Serves 4

Soufflé:

3/4 pound (350 g) pike fillet
without skin, bone, or ends
3 slices homemade-type
sandwich bread
1/4 cup (50 ml) very cold milk
1 1/4 cups (250 g) very
cold heavy cream, 1 egg
1 1/2 tablespoons (20 g)
butter at room temperature
fine sea salt
coarse sea salt or rock salt and
ice cubes for the ice bath
soft butter to butter the molds

Sauce:

1 shallot, 1 carrot
3 - 4 ounces (100 g)
celery root (celeriac)
2 tablespoons olive oil
1/2 teaspoon tomato paste
2 - 3 tablespoons (40 ml) cognac
1/4 cup plus 1 tablespoon
(60 ml) Madeira
3 cups (3/4 liter) shrimp stock
(p. 171)
1/4 teaspoon (1 knife point)
mild curry
2 garlic cloves halved, green germ
removed, and flattened
2 tablespoons finely minced
tarragon leaves
1 thin strip of orange zest (orange
skin with none of the white pith)
4 tablespoons (60 g) butter
6 saffron filaments, fine sea salt
Cayenne pepper
3 tablespoons whipped cream

Final glaze:

2 egg yolks
1/2 cup (100 g) heavy cream
4 tablespoons (40 g) freshly grated
Parmigiano-Reggiano cheese
a few sprigs of chervil

Soufflé:

Rinse the pike fillet in cold water, dry, cut it into cubes, and reserve covered in plastic wrap in the refrigerator. Remove the crust from the slices of sandwich bread and crumble them coarsely. Let them soak in the milk in the refrigerator. Put the cold pike flesh in the bowl of a food processor and process finely. Press the breadcrumbs between your hands, add them to the pike, and process again. Little by little, pour the cold heavy cream continuously into the mixture with the food processor running until you obtain a smooth cream. Finally, incorporate the egg and soft butter. Pass the forcemeat through a fine sieve.

Prepare the ice bath: put the ice cubes and a good handful of salt in a large bowl and fill halfway with cold water. In a smaller bowl, put two tablespoons of forcemeat and mix it with half a teaspoon of fine salt using a rubber spatula. Incorporate the rest of the forcemeat, tablespoon by tablespoon, beating the mixture well to obtain a homogenous, shiny, and flexible forcemeat mixture. Check the seasoning.

Butter four soufflé ramekins of $^{3}/_{4}$ cup (150 ml) capacity and fill each $^{2}/_{3}$ of the way with the forcemeat. Smooth the surfaces. Steam them in a pot fitted with a steamer over boiling water for 15 to 18 minutes until the forcemeat has inflated somewhat and is hot in the interior. Take the warm soufflés and unmold them into a buttered gratin dish.

Sauce:

Peel the shallot, the carrot and the celery root, chop finely and sauté them for a few minutes in a saucepan with the olive oil. Add the tomato paste, stir well and flame the vegetables with the cognac and Madeira. Let the alcohol reduce completely and add the shrimp stock. Add the curry, the cloves of garlic, tarragon and the thin strip of orange peel, and reduce by half over medium heat. Pass the sauce through a sieve, pressing well to extract all the juices. Blend the sauce with an immersion blender or hand mixer, adding the butter in small pieces. Add the saffron filaments and let them infuse for a moment. Season the sauce with the salt and Cayenne pepper.
Right before serving the soufflés, incorporate the whipped cream.

Final Glaze and completion:

Preheat the oven to 350°F (180°C). Combine well the egg yolks, the heavy cream and the Parmigiano- Reggiano. Glaze the unmolded soufflés with the glaze using a pastry brush and brown in the preheated oven for 6 to 8 minutes until they are well puffed and golden.

Pour a little sauce into four hot soup plates. Take the soufflés from the oven and place them, using an offset spatula, on the sauce. Garnish with chervil sprigs and serve immediately.

MUSSELS WITH FRENCH FRIES
«MOULES FRITES»

Serves 4

Mussels:
8 pounds (4 kg) mussels
1 carrot
$^1/_4$ pound (100 g)
celery root (celeriac)
1 celery stalk
1 leek (white and pale green
part only)
fine sea salt
4 tablespoons (60 g) butter
2 cups ($^1/_2$ liter) dry white wine
1 cup (200 g) heavy cream
freshly ground pepper

French Fries:
2 pounds (1 kg) large potatoes
(Russets or Idaho potatoes)
neutral vegetable oil for deep-frying

Completion:
fine sea salt
$^1/_2$ teaspoon finely cut
tarragon leaves
2 tablespoons finely minced chives

Mussels:

Carefully wash the mussels in very cold or ice water, scrape well and trim off the beards. Discard any half-opened mussels.

Peel carrot and celery root. Slice initially into thin lengthwise slices using a mandoline (Benrinder), then into lengthwise sticks and finally into very small cubes (brunoise). Clean the celery stalk and the leek white, wash and dry them, and also cut them in brunoise. Sauté the brunoise 3 to 4 minutes in 1 tablespoon (20 g) of the butter on medium heat in a pot large enough to hold the mussels. Add the white wine, bring to a boil and add the mussels. Cook, covered, 4 to 5 minutes, stirring twice, until the shells open. Take them out using a skimmer and discard any unopened mussels.

Reduce the cooking juices by half, add the cream, let it boil for a minute and incorporate the remaining butter in small pieces in the sauce using a whisk. Season with salt and pepper.

French Fries:

Heat the oil (approximately 2 to 3 quarts/liters) in a fryer to 325°F (160 - 170°C). Peel and cut the potatoes into 2 $^1/_2$ - 3 inches (6 to 7 cm) long and $^1/_2$ inch (1 cm) wide fries. Wash well, drain, and dry them on a towel. Fry (blanch) the potatoes, in small batches, for about 10 minutes, until they are tender. At this point there should be very little coloration on the potatoes. Remove the fries to a sheet tray lined with absorbent paper. Continue until all of the potatoes have been blanched.

Completion:

When ready to serve, heat the oil to 375°F (190°C). Fry the once-cooked potatoes, again in small batches, for about 2 to 3 minutes until they are deep golden brown and crispy. Take the basket from the fryer and shake to remove as much fat as possible. Drain on absorbent paper towels. Repeat until all fries are cooked. Season with salt and gently toss them to distribute the salt well.

Heat the sauce, add the mussels and reheat them. Strew with the tarragon and chives and combine well. Serve them in a large hot dish or soup plates accompanied by the French fries.

MEATS AND POULTRY

VIANDES ET VOLAILLES

SADDLE OF LAMB "BOCUSE D'OR"
SELLE D'AGNEAU «BOCUSE D'OR»

Serves 4

Lamb:
1 ³/4 pounds (800 g)
russet potatoes (4 large)
¹/4 cup neutral vegetable oil
2 tablespoons
coarsely chopped parsley
12 - 16 ounces (400 - 500 g)
saddle of lamb, boned
fine sea salt
freshly ground pepper
¹/2 cup (50 g) bread crumbs

Sauce:
2 cups (¹/2 liter)
lamb stock (p. 173)
1 fresh rosemary sprig
3 tablespoons (50 g) cold butter
fine sea salt

Lamb:

Peel the potatoes, julienne them with a mandoline (Benrinder) and press them well between your hands to rid them of excess moisture. Heat 2 tablespoons of oil in a large non-stick frying pan. Spread out half of the potatoes in a thin layer to make a large wafer-thin pancake (galette) of 10 inches (24 cm) in diameter. Brown on medium heat on one side and slip it onto a cloth without turning it over. Strew on half of the chopped parsley. Repeat the operation for the second galette.

Preheat the oven to 425°F (220°C).

Cut the saddle of lamb in half to obtain two equal 8 inch (20 cm) pieces. Dry the pieces well with absorbent paper towels and season with salt and pepper. Roll lightly in the bread crumbs. Place each piece on a potato galette and roll up the pancake using the cloth. Close the edges of the galette and place them on a rack. Cook the saddles of lamb in the preheated oven for 15 minutes.

Sauce:

Add the rosemary to the lamb stock, heat and reduce to half, and then discard the rosemary. Thicken the sauce with the butter: add the butter in small pieces and incorporate by swirling the pan. Check the seasoning of the sauce.

To serve:

Take the lamb out of the oven and slice each into four pieces. Place two pieces per person on a hot plate and serve with the sauce passed separately.

VEAL MILANESE
ESCALOPE DE VEAU MILANAISE

Serves 4

Veal scallops:
2 eggs
fine sea salt
freshly ground pepper
8 small veal scallops
(taken from the topside)
about 2 ounces (60 g) each
$^{1}/_{2}$ cup (60 - 80 g) flour
4 cups (150 g) freshly grated
bread crumbs
2 ounces (50 g) finely and freshly
grated Parmigiano-Reggiano cheese
approximately 7 tablespoons
(100 g) clarified butter (p. 169)
2 - 3 tablespoons (40 g) butter

To serve:
$^{1}/_{2}$ organic or unwaxed lemon

Scallops:
Whip eggs and 1 tablespoon of water, salt and pepper the mixture lightly, and pour it in a soup plate. Dry the veal scallops with absorbent paper towels and flatten them a little between two sheets of plastic wrap. Season on both sides. Put the flour on a plate. Mix the bread crumbs and the Parmigiano-Reggiano on another plate.
To bread the scallops, flour them on both sides, shake a little in order to remove the surplus of flour, dip them quickly in the beaten eggs, and roll them in the Parmigiano-bread crumb mixture without pressing too firmly on the breading.

Heat a good quantity of clarified butter in a large frying pan on medium heat. Add the breaded scallops in one layer. Brown them on the first side by lifting the edges once, so that the butter can spread uniformly. Turn them over, add the fresh butter and continue cooking until obtaining uniformly golden browned and crispy scallops.

To serve:
Take the veal from the frying pan; drain them for an instant on absorbent paper towels and season with salt. Serve accompanied by a lemon wedge and a small rocked salad.

THICK VEAL STEAKS WITH FRIED SAGE LEAVES
PAVÉS DE VEAU AUX FEUILLES DE SAUGE FRITES

Serves 4

Sage leaves:
neutral vegetable oil for deep-frying
20 well-shaped sage leaves
of average size
fine sea salt

Veal Steaks:
4 veal steaks (taken from the loin)
1 1/4 - 1 1/2 inches (3 to 4 cm)
thick, about 6 ounces (180 g)
each fine sea salt
freshly ground pepper
3 tablespoons (50 g) butter
1 garlic clove
4 sage leaves

Sauce:
1/3 cup (80 ml) Marsala
2 1/2 cup (600 ml) veal stock
(p. 173)
1 tablespoon (20 g) butter
fine sea salt
freshly ground pepper

To serve:
4 - 5 tablespoons pea purée
(p. 122)

Sage leaves:

Heat the oil in a fryer or a large frying pan with high sides to 320 - 340°F (160 - 170°C). Wash the sage leaves, dry carefully and fry them for 20 seconds, one after the other (be careful, the oil is likely to splatter!). Take out the leaves with a skimmer when they are crisp but still quite green. Press immediately between two absorbent paper towels to flatten them.

Veal steaks:

Slightly flatten the steaks with the palm of your hand and season them. Heat the butter in a large cast-iron casserole until it foams. As soon as butter stops foaming, put in the steaks and sear on the first side for 7 to 8 minutes, then turn them over. Add the garlic clove and place a sage leaf on each steak. To obtain medium steaks, continue cooking 4 to 5 minutes. During the cooking, baste the steaks regularly with the butter. Take the meat and the garlic clove out of the casserole, place the steaks on a rack and let them rest in a preheated 125°F (50°C, warm) oven.

Sauce:

Degrease the casserole, reserving the cooking butter. Deglaze with the Marsala and let it reduce to a syrup. Add the veal stock and let it reduce to a third (this reduction can be made in advance). Pass the sauce base through a fine sieve and add the cooking butter and the fresh butter. Let the butter melt into the sauce without incorporating it. Season the sauce with salt and pepper to taste.

To serve:

Heat the puréed peas in a small pan on low heat. Place the steaks in the center of four hot plates, garnish with a good tablespoon of pea purée and three fried sage leaves. Pour a ribbon of sauce around the steak. Serve accompanied by blanched snow peas and little long, white radishes glazed in butter.

CALVES' SWEETBREADS SKEWERS WITH BUTTERED CROÛTONS
BROCHETTES DE RIS DE VEAU AUX CROÛTONS BEURRÉS

Serves 4

Skewers:

*(to be prepared
one day in advance)*
*4 pieces calves' sweetbread,
rather long, 5 ounces (150 g)
each, cleaned*
fine sea salt
freshly ground pepper
4 long bamboo or wooden skewers

Sauce:

2 shallots
3 - 4 small, cultivated mushrooms
3 tablespoons (50 g) butter
fine sea salt
¹/4 cup (40 ml) balsamic vinegar
*2 tablespoons (20 ml)
Sherry vinegar*
³/4 cup (200 ml) Ruby Port
*1 cup (¹/4 liter)
veal stock (p. 173)*
*1 cup (¹/4 liter)
chicken stock (p. 172)*

Croûtons:

*6 slices homemade-type
sandwich bread*
*7 tablespoons (100 g) clarified
butter (p. 169)*

Skewers:

Soak the sweetbreads in several changes of cold water, a few hours or overnight, until the water remains clear. Remove the sweetbreads from the water, dry them, eliminate the thin membrane that covers them and trim them into long pieces 1¹/2 - 2 inches (4 - 5 cm) in width. Salt and pepper them. Roll each piece in a sheet of plastic wrap and form them in 1 x 5 inch (2 x 12 cm) long rolls by tightening them well. Tie the ends. Plunge the rolls in boiling water, lower the heat and poach them approximately 10 to 12 minutes by covering them with a towel soaked in the poaching water, so that they remain under the water. Take them out of the water and shock them in ice water. Remove the plastic wrap from the cooled rolls and slice into 1/2 inch (1 cm) slices. Thread the slices on four skewers. Reserve in the refrigerator.

Sauce:

Peel the shallots and slice them. Clean the mushrooms, if necessary wipe them with a damp towel, and slice finely. Sauté the shallots and mushrooms in a small pan in 1 tablespoon (15 g) of butter until translucent. Salt lightly and deglaze with the two vinegars. Add the Port and let it reduce to a syrup. Add the two stocks and let reduce by a third. Pass the sauce through a fine strainer and thicken by adding the butter in small pieces. Season with salt and pepper.

Croûtons:

Prepare croûtons as described on p. 24 and put them in an oval gratin dish.

Completion:

Preheat the broiler. Heat the skewers 8 to 10 minutes in the sauce simmering on low heat, basting often. If the sauce becomes too thick, thin it out with a little water or stock. Take the skewers from the sauce, drain them for a moment and then roll them in the croûtons. Arrange in a buttered gratin dish and sprinkle generously with the remaining croûtons. Brown the skewers for a few minutes under the heated broiler so that the croûtons become quite crisp. Place them on hot plates. Check the seasoning of the sauce and pour a ribbon of sauce around the skewers. Serve the skewers of calves' sweetbreads accompanied by sautéed mushrooms and mashed potatoes (p. 120).

ROLLED ROAST OF SUCKLING PIGLET, MARJORAM SAUCE

RÔTI DE PORCELET ROULÉ, SAUCE MARJOLAINE

Serves 4

Sauce base:

(to be prepared 1 day in advance)
1 carrot
$^1/_4$ pound (120 g)
celery root (celeriac)
1 onion , 1 white of leek
bones from the pork loin, chopped,
or 2 $^1/_4$ pounds (1 kg) veal bones
2 tablespoons oil
$^1/_2$ teaspoon tomato paste
$^1/_2$ cup (0.125 liter)
dry white wine
5 garlic cloves
1 bay leaf (laurel)
3 marjoram sprigs

Roast:

1 $^3/_4$ pounds (800 g) of boned loin
of suckling or very young piglet
with the skin intact
(to order at your butcher)
fine sea salt
$^1/_2$ teaspoon coarsely ground
black pepper
2 tablespoons chopped parsley
1 tablespoon minced
marjoram leaves
2 tablespoons (30 g) soft butter
1 teaspoon olive oil
1 onion , 8 garlic cloves
3 fresh thyme sprigs
approximately 1 cup ($^1/_4$ liter)
of sauce base (see above)

Completion:

2 tablespoons (30 g) butter
fine sea salt
freshly ground pepper
1 tablespoon finely minced
marjoram leaves

Sauce base:

Peel and clean the vegetables, wash them and cut into $^1/_2$ inch (2 cm) pieces (mirepoix). Sauté the bones in 1 tablespoon of oil in a pot over high heat until they have a beautiful brown color. Take them out of the pan and drain them in a strainer. Degrease the pan, sauté the vegetables 3 to 4 minutes, add the bones and the tomato paste while stirring. Deglaze with the white wine, let it reduce to a syrup and cover with water. Add the garlic, the bay leaf, and the sprigs of marjoram. Let the base simmer for 2 hours over low heat. If necessary add water. Pass the liquid through a fine-meshed sieve, pressing well to extract all the juices. Let it cool overnight in the refrigerator. The following day, degrease carefully by removing all of the fat that has hardened on the surface.

Roast:

Rinse the pork loin with cold water and dry it with absorbent paper towels. Salt the interior of the roast and sprinkle it with the black pepper and chopped herbs. Roll it so that the skin side is out and tie it every inch (2 cm) or so with kitchen twine to obtain a round roast. with a pastry brush baste the surface of the roast with melted butter and salt. Preheat the oven to 425°F (220°C). If you have one, oil a spit-roaster or a deep roasting pan. Peel the onion, quarter it and distribute the onion, the garlic cloves and the thyme in the bottom of the spit-roaster or pan. Place the roast into the roaster with the cut side down. Pour the sauce base in the bottom of the roaster and place in the oven. Roast 1 to 1 $^1/_2$ hours, basting the pork loin with its juices, until it is quite hot inside and crusty outside. The roast is cooked when you prick the roast with a skewer and the cooking juices run clear.

Completion:

For the sauce, measure 2 $^1/_2$ cups (600 ml) of the sauce base and reduce it to a third. With an immersion blender or hand mixer blend the juices, adding butter in small pieces to bind it. Season it with salt and pepper and add the minced marjoram. Take the roast out of the oven, place it on a rack (or leave it on the one that it cooked on) and let it rest 10 minutes before slicing it. Remove the string, slice the meat in $^3/_4$ inch (2 cm) slices and place them on hot plates. Serve the sauce out of a sauceboat.

BEEF TENDERLOIN STEAKS WITH RED WINE SAUCE

FILET DE BŒUF POÊLÉ, SAUCE AU VIN ROUGE

Serves 4

Garnish:
neutral vegetable oil for deep-frying
2 medium onions
1 - 2 tablespoons sifted flour
fine sea salt

Sauce:
4 shallots
3/4 cup (200 ml)
full-bodied red wine
1 fresh thyme sprig
3 - 4 small cultivated mushrooms
3 1/2 tablespoons (50 g) butter
1 pinch of sugar
1 cup (1/4 liter)
veal stock (p. 173)
1 cup (1/4 liter)
chicken stock (p. 172)
fine sea salt

Steaks:
4 tenderloin / filet steaks,
1 1/2 - 2 inches thick (4 - 5cm),
6 1/2 ounces (200g) each
fine sea salt
freshly ground pepper
4 tablespoons (60 g) butter

To serve:
Mixed fried herb leaves,
for example: flat-leaf parsley,
sage, basil (p. 170)

Garnish:

Heat the oil in a fryer to 325°F (160°C). Peel the onions, slice in fine, regular 2/3 inch (2 mm) slices and separate the rings. Use only well-shaped rings. Flour lightly in a strainer. Shake well to remove excess flour. Fry the rings in small batches in the hot oil until they have a beautiful golden color. Take them out with the basket and drain them on absorbent paper towels. Salt.

Sauce:

For the red wine reduction, peel 3 of the shallots, slice them and put them, the red wine, and the thyme in a small saucepan. Bring to the boil and let the wine reduce almost to a syrup. Remove the thyme.

For the sauce, peel the remaining shallot and mince. Clean the mushrooms, if necessary wipe them with a damp paper towel, and slice them. Heat the shallot and mushrooms in a small pan with the butter over a low heat until the turn golden. Add a pinch of sugar and caramelize lightly. Add the two stocks and let them reduce to a third. Pour in the red wine reduction, let it simmer for a few minutes, and then pass the sauce through a fine-meshed sieve. Thicken the sauce with the butter by adding the butter in small pieces. Season with salt and pepper. Reserve the sauce over very low heat.

Steaks:

Tie the filet steaks horizontally to give them a nice shape with a kitchen twine. Flatten them a little with the palm of your hand. Heat the butter in a cast-iron casserole until it foams. Salt and pepper the steaks. Place them in the casserole as soon as the butter has stopped foaming. Pan-fry on both sides, 12 to 14 minutes in all for medium-rare steaks. Lift them with a fork from time to time so that the butter can be well distributed. During cooking, baste with the butter so that they cook regularly and get crunchy-brown on the outside. Remove the casserole from the heat and let the meat rest in the casserole a moment longer. Remove the twine.

To serve:

Place the steaks on heated plates and garnish with a generous portion of onions and fried herbs. Pour a ribbon of sauce around the steaks and serve accompanied by mashed potatoes (p. 120).

FRENCH-STYLE BOILED BEEF, HORSERADISH-APPLE SAUCE
POT AU FEU DE BŒUF, SAUCE RAIFORT-POMME

Serves 4 to 6

Boiled Beef:
1 3/4 pounds (800 g)
beef blade or silverside
sea salt
2 medium onions
2 cloves
1 tomato
1 bay leaf (laurel)
5 parsley sprigs
1 fresh thyme sprig
1 leek leaf, 6 - 8 inch
(15 - 20 cm) long
4 garlic cloves
1 teaspoon black peppercorns
3 medium carrots
2 leeks (white and pale
green parts only)
8 celery stalks

Sauce:
4 tablespoons
mayonnaise (p. 168)
6 - 8 tablespoons finely and
freshly grated horseradish
4 tablespoons crème fraîche
or sour cream
1 tart apple (Granny Smith)
fine sea salt
freshly ground pepper
a few drops fresh lemon juice

To serve:
fleur de sel or coarse sea salt

Boiled Beef:

Wash beef under a stream of cold water, place it in a pot and cover with cold water, measuring the water as you do so. Add a teaspoon (5 g) of salt per quart (liter) of water.

Halve an onion horizontally and arrange sliced side down in a sauté pan, without oil, on medium heat. Brown for 4 to 5 minutes until they are very brown (almost black) and caramelized, in order to give flavor and color to the broth. Peel the second onion, slice in half and stud with the cloves. Wash the tomato and slice. Make a bouquet garni by wrapping the bay leaf, parsley, and thyme in the leek leaf, and tying with twine. Place the onions, tomato, garlic, and bouquet garni into the pot with the beef. Boil the meat 3 1/2 to 4 hours at a bare simmer on low heat until the beef is very tender. Skim the broth from time to time so that it becomes quite clear.

Peel the carrots and slice diagonally in 1/4 inch (1/2 cm) slices. Clean the leeks, halve lengthwise, wash, shake dry and cut into 4 inch (10 cm) pieces. Peel the celery stalks with a vegetable peeler to remove the strings and cut into 4 inch (10 cm) pieces. Add the vegetables 1 hour before the beef is done. If need be, remove the vegetables earlier if you prefer them not too tender.

Sauce:

Combine the mayonnaise, horseradish, and the crème fraîche or sour cream to a smooth cream. Peel the apple, quarter, remove the seeds, grate finely and mix with the sauce. If the sauce appears too thick, thin it with a little heavy cream. Season it with salt, pepper and a few drops of lemon juice to taste.

To serve:

Take the meat, carrots, celery, and leek out of the broth. Pass the broth through a fine strainer and allow it to cool in order to degrease it. You can serve the broth piping hot on the side with the beef or use it as a base for the consommé (p. 28).

Cut the beef in slices. Arrange the slices with the vegetables on a large heated platter and sprinkle the meat with a little fleur de sel. Serve the boiled beef accompanied by the horseradish-apple sauce.

ROASTED CHICKEN SERVED IN TWO SERVICES
POULARDE AU FOUR EN DEUX SERVICES

Serves 2 to 3

Chicken:
1 free-range chicken/roaster,
2 1/2 - 3 1/2 pounds (1,2 - 1,5 kg)
2 - 3 tablespoons (30 - 40 g)
soft butter
fine sea salt
freshly ground pepper

First service:
1/2 quart (1/2 liter)
chicken stock (p. 172)
1 marjoram sprig
1/3 cup (80 g) heavy cream
1 1/2 tablespoons (20 g)
cold butter
fine sea salt

Second service:
3 - 4 ounces (80 - 100 g,
two large handfuls) mixed salad
and fresh herb leaves (e. g.,
chervil, flat-leaf parsley, basil)
5 tablespoons of elegant
vinaigrette (p. 168)

To serve:
approximately 3 ounces (100 g)
fresh tagliatelle (p. 175)
sea salt
1 tablespoon (15 g) butter
2 - 3 tablespoons whipped cream
fleur de sel or coarse sea salt
parsley oil for drizzling (p. 169)

Chicken :

Preheat the oven to 400°F (200°C). Rinse the chicken under a stream of cold water and dry carefully. Rub the chicken all over with the soft butter. Salt and pepper it inside and out. Place it on a rack in a roasting pan to facilitate basting while it is roasted. Roast the chicken in the pre-heated oven for 45 to 50 minutes, depending on its size, so that it is golden brown and crisp. The chicken is cooked when the juices run out clear. Take the chicken out of the oven and place it breast side down on the rack. Let it rest for ten minutes. Keep warm.

First service:

Reduce the chicken stock to a third with the sprig of marjoram. Remove the marjoram, pour in the cream and thicken the sauce by adding the butter in small pieces. Season with salt.

Second service:

Pick through the salad and the herb leaves, wash and dry them. Check the seasoning of the vinaigrette.

To serve:

Carve the chicken. Remove the wings and divide the breast into 2 or 3 pieces. Place the legs, thighs and wings on an oiled heat-proof plate or grilling pan and reserve.

Preheat the broiler. For the first service, cook the tagliatelle in boiling salted water. Drain, but reserve a little of the cooking water. Put the tagliatelle in a sauté pan, add 2 - 3 tablespoons of the cooking water and the butter (if you want, you can add a julienne of fresh black truffle) and keep warm over low heat. Blend the sauce to make it foam and incorporate the whipped cream. Divide the chicken breast and the fresh pasta among two or three plates, coat with the sauce, and serve.

For the second service, brown the legs, thighs, and wings for a few minutes under the pre-heated broiler to make them quite crisp. Meanwhile, toss the salad with the vinaigrette and arrange in small bouquets on 2 or 3 plates. Pour a ribbon of parsley oil around. Salt the chicken pieces with fleur de sel, place them alongside the salad, and serve immediately.

YOUNG RABBIT BRAISED WITH JUNIPER BERRIES

LAPEREAU BRAISÉ AUX BAIES DE GENIÈVRE

Serves 3 to 4

Rabbit:
1 young rabbit,
about 3 pounds (1,5 kg)
fine sea salt
freshly ground pepper
2 teaspoons (10 g) butter
1 - 2 tablespoons olive oil
1 pinch of brown sugar
juice of half an orange
approximately 3 cups (³/4 liter)
chicken stock (p. 172)
6 slightly crushed juniper berries
2 thin strips of orange zest
(orange part only,
with none of the white pith)

Vegetables:
Approximately 1³/4 pounds
(800 g) of assorted small
vegetables of the season
(for example: peas, snow peas,
baby carrots, small white
bulb onions, baby spinach,
broad beans…)
sea salt
1 - 2 tablespoons (20 g) butter
freshly ground pepper

Completion:
fine sea salt
freshly ground pepper
4 tablespoons (60 g) butter
¹/4 cup (50 g) heavy cream
2 - 3 tablespoons whipped cream

Rabbit:

Disjoint the rabbit by removing the front and back legs. Divide the thighs and the legs in two at the joints. Bone the saddle and reserve fillets covered with plastic wrap in the refrigerator. Cut the skin of the sides in two and knot them in order to obtain four small parcels. Chop the bones coarsely.

Salt and pepper the thighs, legs and sides. Brown the pieces of meat and the bones in a large cast iron casserole in oil and butter over high heat, adding a pinch of brown sugar to caramelize them. Deglaze with the orange juice and add chicken stock to cover. Add the juniper berries and the orange zest. Braise the pieces of young rabbit, covered, over low heat for a good hour until the meat is tender. Take the meat from the casserole and pass the cooking juices through a fine-meshed sieve.

Vegetables:

Depending on the vegetable, clean or peel them, wash them and, if necessary, halve or slice. Cook the vegetables, one after the other, in boiling, salted water and shock them in salted ice water. Drain them and dry with absorbent paper towels. At the time of serving, briefly sauté them with butter in a sauté pan over low heat. Season with salt and pepper.

Completion:

For the sauce, reduce ²/3 of the cooking juices in a small pan by half. Add the cream and whisk in the butter in small pieces to bind it. Season. Heat the pieces of young rabbit in the remaining cooking juices.

Salt and pepper the fillets of young rabbit. Heat 1 ¹/2 tablespoons (20 g) of butter in a small sauté pan. Arrange the fillets in the pan and sear them for 4 to 5 minutes, turning them once to brown both sides. Remove the sauté pan from the heat, but allow the fillets to rest in the retained heat for a moment. Slice the fillets on the diagonal into ¹/2 inch (1 cm) slices.

Blend the sauce to make it foam and incorporate the whipped cream. Arrange nicely a piece of thigh and a piece of shoulder, 2 to 3 sections of fillet and an assortment of vegetables per person on each of four hot plates. Coat with the sauce and serve.

VEGETABLES AND SIDE DISHES
LÉGUMES ET GARNITURES

RED BEET PURÉE AND SYRUP
PURÉE DE BETTERAVES ROUGES ET SON SIROP

Serves 6 to 8 in accompaniment
with cold meat patés or foie gras
terrine on p. 40

Purée:
10 ounces (300 g) red beets
sea salt
a pinch of sugar
3 1/2 tablespoons (50 g) butter
balsamic vinegar for seasoning
1 teaspoon olive oil

Garnish:
neutral vegetable oil for deep-frying
well shaped sage leaves
of average size
fine sea salt

Purée:

Peel the beets, protecting your hands with disposable plastic gloves. Slice into 1/2 - 3/4 inch (1 - 2 cm) slices, wash and place them in a small pan. Cover with cold water. Add salt and a good pinch of sugar. Cook for 45 to 55 minutes at a bare simmer, until the beets are very tender. Drain and reserve the cooking liquid. Let the beets cool a little, then purée the pieces, adding the butter and then the oil at the end. When the purée is smooth, adjust the seasoning and add balsamic vinegar to taste. Pass the purée through a fine sieve using a scraper, let it cool completely and put it in a pastry bag fitted with a large round tip.

For the syrup, reduce the cooking liquid in a small pan on medium heat until it has a syrupy consistency. Let cool and pour into bottle with a fine plastic nozzle to facilitate plate decoration.

Garnish:

Heat enough oil to 325 - 350°F (160 - 170°C) in a fryer or a large frying pan with a high rim. Wash the sage leaves, dry carefully and fry them for 20 seconds one after the other (be careful, the oil is likely to splatter!). Take out the leaves with a skimmer when they are crisp but still green. Press immediately between two absorbent paper towels to flatten them.

To serve:

Squeeze a small portion of purée onto each plate and garnish with one or more fried sage leaves. You can also garnish the plates with a ribbon of syrup which complements the taste of most meat patés and foie gras.

MY FAVORITE POTATOES
MES POMMES DE TERRE PRÉFÉRÉES

Serves 4

Potatoes:
1 ³/4 pounds (800 g)
of your favorite potatoes
(for example: Russet or Idaho)
sea salt
¹/4 - ¹/3 cup (70 - 80 ml)
extra-virgin olive oil
fleur de sel or coarse sea salt
2 - 3 tablespoons coarsely chopped
flat-leaf parsley

Potatoes:
Peel the potatoes, wash, and halve or quarter them depending on their size. Steam them over salted water until they start to break up. In a pan, heat two tablespoons of water. Add the potatoes, olive oil, a little fleur de sel, and the chopped parsley. With a fork coarsely crush/mash everything together, working quickly. Check the seasoning and serve the crushed potatoes in heated bowls.

Note:
Depending on the dish you want to serve the potatoes with, you can substitute melted butter for the olive oil.

MASHED POTATOES
PURÉE DE POMMES DE TERRE

Serves 4

Mashed potatoes:
2 pounds (1 kg)
waxy gold potatoes
(for example: Yukon gold)
sea salt
1 ^{1}/$_4$ - 1 ^{1}/$_2$ cups (300 - 350 ml)
full-fat milk
1 - 1 ^{1}/$_2$ sticks (140 - 160 g) butter

Mashed potatoes:

Scrub the skins of the potatoes. Put them, whole, in a pan and cover them with cold water. Add salt, bring to the boil, and cook at a slow boil until a knife pierces them easily. Warm the milk.

Drain the cooked potatoes, peel them while still hot and pass them through the fine blade of a food mill into a pan. Pour the hot milk evenly over the pulp while stirring vigorously with a wooden spatula. Add just enough milk to obtain smooth but still firm mashed potatoes. Mix in half of the butter, in small pieces. Then pass the mashed potatoes through a fine sieve using a scraper and return them to the pan.
Check the seasoning.

To serve, heat the mashed potatoes over low heat, stirring constantly. Add the remaining butter, incorporating it well to produce a smooth texture. Serve it onto hot plates. If desired, garnish with chervil sprigs.

Note:

If you want to prepare the mashed potatoes in advance, cover with three layers of plastic wrap to prevent the surface from crusting over.

GREEN PEA PURÉE WITH HAZELNUT OIL
PURÉE DE PETITS POIS À L'HUILE DE NOISETTE

Serves 4

Purée:

1 pound (500 g) shelled green peas
(that is to say, 2 - 2 ¹/₂ pounds
or 1 - 1,2 kg in the pod)
sea salt
a pinch of sugar
¹/₂ cup (100 g) heavy cream
a little chicken stock (p. 172)
3 - 4 tablespoons (50 g) butter
¹/₄ cup (60 ml) virgin hazelnut oil

Purée:

Cook the peas approximately 5 minutes in boiling salted water with a good pinch of added sugar. Drain, and blend with the cream into a fine purée. If the purée appears too thick, add a little more cream or some chicken stock. Mix in the butter in small pieces. Finally, pour in the hazelnut oil.

Check the seasoning and pass the purée through a very fine sieve with the aid of a scraper. Place in a pan and heat over low heat while stirring. Serve the purée of peas in a heated bowl.

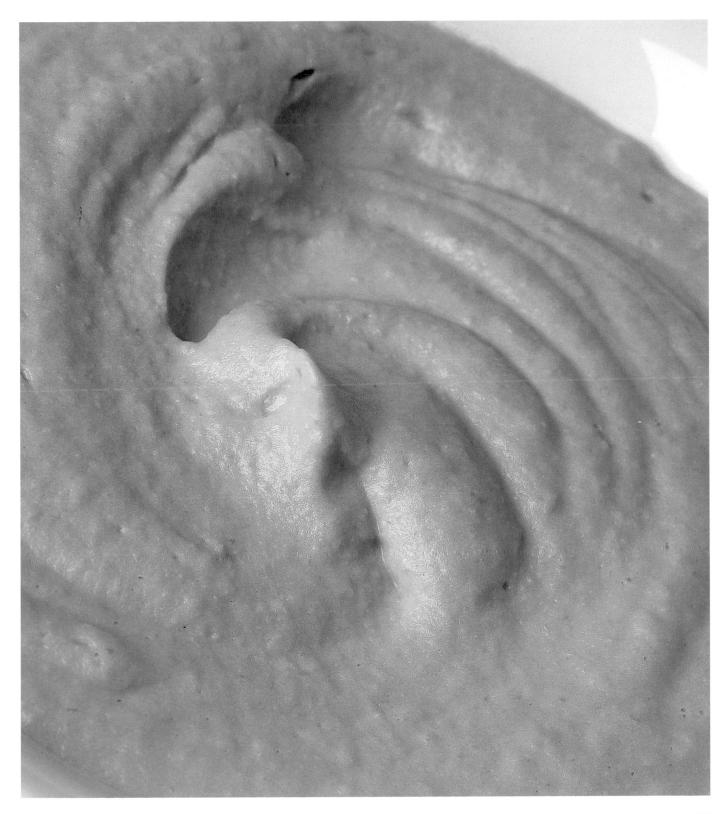

WHITE BEAN PURÉE
PURÉE DE COCOS BLANCS

Serves 6 to 8

Purée:
¹/₂ pound (250 g)
dried white beans
1 quart (1 liter)
chicken stock (p. 172)
1 bay leaf (laurel)
3 parsley sprigs
1 fresh thyme sprig
1 leek leaf, 6 - 8 inch
(15 - 20 cm) long
¹/₂ an onion
2 garlic cloves, peeled

For serving:
¹/₂ cup (100 g) heavy cream
4 tablespoons (60 g) butter
fine sea salt
extra-virgin olive oil

Purée:

Wash the white beans in several changes of cold water, drain them and place them in a large pan. Pour in a quart of chicken stock and bring to the boil. Make a bouquet garni by wrapping the bay leaf, parsley, and thyme in the leek leaf, and tying with kitchen twine. Peel the half onion. Halve the garlic cloves and remove the green germs. Add the bouquet garni, the onion and the garlic to the pan with the beans and stock. Cook the beans at a slow boil for a good hour until they are very tender. If necessary, add a little more liquid.

Remove and discard the herbs. Remove the beans and drain, reserving the cooking broth. Blend the beans into a fine purée, adding a little cooking broth. Add as much broth as necessary to obtain a smooth but relatively firm purée. Pass the purée through a very fine sieve with the aid of a scraper and return it to a pan.

To serve:

Heat the purée over low heat while stirring constantly with a wooden spatula. Add in the cream first, then the butter in small pieces. Vigorously mix the purée until it becomes quite creamy. If it appears too thick to you, add a little more cream. Check the seasoning and pour in a fillip of olive oil. Serve the white bean purée piping hot.

CARAMELIZED CARROTS
CAROTTES CARAMÉLISÉES

Serves 4

Carrots:
1 bunch of spring carrots
(approximately 10 small carrots)
5 - 6 tablespoons
(60 - 80 g) butter
fine sea salt
1 pinch of sugar
2 garlic cloves, peeled

For serving:
Sprigs of chervil

Carrots:

Trim the ends off the carrots. Peel carrots and cut diagonally in $^1/_4$ inch ($^1/_2$ cm) slices. Heat the butter in a cast-iron casserole. Add the carrot slices in a single layer. Season with salt and a pinch of sugar. Add the garlic cloves. Cover and cook for seven minutes on a low heat. Remove the cover and turn the carrots. Allow to cook uncovered at for another seven or eight minutes, until the carrots become tender and are well caramelized on both sides.

To serve:

Check the seasoning. Serve the carrots on hot plates and garnish with chervil sprigs.

SAVOY CABBAGE WITH BACON
CHOU VERT FRISÉ AUX LARDONS

Serves 4

Cabbage:
1 small head
(or half a large head)
Savoy cabbage
sea salt
approximately 4 ounces (120 g)
or 8 - 10 very thin slices
of smoked bacon

For serving:
¹/2 cup (100 ml)
chicken stock (p. 172)
7 tablespoons (100 g) cold butter
fine sea salt

Cabbage:

Remove the tough, dark green leaves from the outside of the cabbage. Remove the ribs from the remaining leaves and cut the leaves into 1 inch (3 cm) diamonds. Cook them in boiling salted water. Remove them when they are still crisp (al dente) and shock in salted ice water. Drain, and dry them well between absorbent paper towels.

Cut the bacon slices into thin sticks (lardons). Blanch for a few seconds in unsalted boiling water. Drain, and dry them with absorbent paper towels.

To serve:

Reduce the chicken stock by a third in a saucepan or a frying pan over low heat. Thicken the stock with the butter: to accomplish that, incorporate the cold butter in small pieces while gently swirling the pan to obtain a smooth and shiny emulsification (do not let it boil at any time). Add the cabbage and the bacon, and allow them to reheat in the sauce. Check the seasoning. Serve in a heated bowl.

ARTICHOKES BARIGOULE
BARIGOULE D'ARTICHAUTS

Serves 4 as a first course

Artichokes:
12 small and tender artichokes
with stems
juice of half a lemon
2 shallots
4 average carrots
2 tablespoons olive oil
fine sea salt
freshly ground pepper
$^1/_3$ cup (80 ml) dry white wine
$^1/_2$ cup (0.125 liter)
chicken stock (p. 172)
1 fresh thyme sprig
1 bay leaf (laurel)

For serving:
10 large basil leaves
fine sea salt
freshly ground pepper
extra-virgin olive oil

Artichokes:

Pare and trim the artichokes: i.e., remove the outer dark green leaves until the more tender leaves appear. Cut the remaining leaves off $^1/_2$ inch (1 cm) above the top of the artichoke bottom. Shorten the stem to $1^1/_2$ inches (4 cm). With a small knife, carefully peel the artichoke bottom and, if necessary to be sure that you have removed all of the tough, dark green outer skin, trim the circumference further. Using a teaspoon or a melon baller, remove the choke from the center of the artichoke bottoms, and then halve the artichoke. Reserve the artichokes in water that has been acidified with the lemon juice.

Peel the shallots and mince finely. Peel and halve the carrots, and then cut into 1 to $1^1/_2$ inch (3 to 4 cm) long sticks. Carve the sticks into the shape of an elongated olive using a small knife. Take the artichokes from the water and drain them. Heat the olive oil in a large cast-iron casserole. Add the artichokes, carrots and shallots and heat for 3 to 4 minutes to brown them. Deglaze with the white wine and let the liquid reduce to a syrup. Cover the vegetables with the chicken stock. Add the thyme and the bay leaf. Braise the vegetables covered until they are quite tender at low heat, approximately 12 minutes. After 6 minutes remove the lid so that the cooking liquid can evaporate and the artichokes get a shiny glaze. At the end of cooking, discard the herbs.

To serve:

Cut the basil leaves into a fine julienne. Season the artichokes with salt and pepper and add the basil. Arrange the vegetables in heated soup plates, drizzle with extra-virgin olive oil and serve.

WHITE AND GREEN ASPARAGUS WITH MOREL MUSHROOMS
ASPERGES BLANCHES ET VERTES AUX MORILLES

Serves 4

Asparagus:
12 green asparagus of average size
(approximately 1 - 1 1/4 pounds,
or 500 - 600 g)
12 white asparagus of average size
(approximately 1 - 1 1/4 pounds,
or 500 - c600 g)
1/2 cup chicken stock (p. 172)
fine sea salt
a pinch of sugar

Morels:
11 ounces (300 g)
small fresh morels
1 - 2 tablespoons (20 g) butter
3 tablespoons (40 ml) dry Sherry
(Tio Pepe)
1/2 cup (100 ml)
chicken stock (p. 172)
fine sea salt

For serving:
5 - 6 tablespoons (80 g) butter
3 tablespoons whipped cream

Asparagus:

Cut the asparagus to the same length (approximately 8 inches, or 20 cm) on a board to avoid breaking them. Reserve the cut off pieces of white asparagus. Carefully peel the white asparagus from the tip to the ends. Peel only the tough ends of the green asparagus.

For the sauce, cook the cut-off white asparagus pieces in the chicken stock until they are tender. Purée finely with an immersion blender or food processor, pass the sauce through a fine-meshed sieve and season with salt. Reserve.

Cook the green asparagus approximately 8 to 10 minutes in boiling salted water. Remove when they are still slightly crisp. Shock with salted ice water and drain well.

A quarter hour before serving, cook the white asparagus approximately 12 to 14 minutes in boiling salted water to which a good pinch of sugar has been added. They must be a little more cooked than the green ones.

Morels:

While the white asparagus are cooking, clean the morels. Wash well with cold water, and dry. Halve any large ones and leave the small ones whole. Melt the butter in a hot sauté pan. Add the morels, salt them and allow them to cook for a moment. Deglaze with the sherry and add the chicken stock. Allow the whole to simmer until the liquid is almost evaporated.

To serve:

Heat the green asparagus in a frying pan in 2 tablespoons (30 g) of butter. Melt the remaining butter. Remove the white asparagus from their cooking water using a skimmer and drain them on a kitchen towel.

To dress the plates nicely, alternate 3 green asparagus and 3 white asparagus on each heated plate. Brush the white asparagus with the melted butter. Reheat the asparagus sauce, incorporate the whipped cream and drizzle the tips and bottoms of the asparagus with the sauce. Arrange the morels on the asparagus and serve immediately.

DESSERTS AND PASTRIES

DESSERTS ET PETIT FOURS

CRÈME BRÛLÉE
CRÈME BRÛLÉE

CRÈME BRÛLÉE

Serves 4 to 6

Crème:
$^2/_3$ cup (160 ml) full-fat milk
$1^1/_2$ cups (300 g) heavy cream
$2^1/_2$ ounces (80 g) sugar
4 egg yolks
1 vanilla bean

To serve:
4 - 6 tablespoons brown sugar

Cream:

Combine the milk, cream, sugar and egg yolks well with a whisk. Split the vanilla bean lengthwise and scrape out the seeds using a small knife. Add the bean and its seeds to the preceding preparation. Let it rest for a few hours or, better, overnight, covered with plastic wrap in the refrigerator.

Preheat the oven to 200 - 225°F (100°C).

Pass the crème brûlée mixture through a fine sieve and divide it into 4 or 6 small porcelain dishes (depending on their size). Cook the creams for 1 hour in the preheated oven, until they just "tremble" in the center when you move them. Take them out of the oven, let them cool.

To serve:

Dust the creams with a fine layer of brown sugar. Caramelize the sugar using a blowtorch and serve the crèmes brûlées at once.

ROSEMARY-LIME ICE CREAM MERINGUÉ
GLACES AU ROMARIN ET CITRON VERT MERINGUÉES

Serves 8 to 10

Ice cream:
(makes about 1¹/₄ pints/ ³/₄ liter)
8 - 10 stemmed glasses
(martini, or other)
with ¹/₂ cup (120 ml) capacity
1¹/₂ cups (300 g) heavy cream
2 cups (400 ml) full-fat milk
1¹/₂ ounces (50 g)
fresh rosemary leaves
4 organic or unwaxed limes
²/₃ cup (150 g) sugar

Meringue:
4 egg whites (120 g)
2 ¹/₂ cups (250 g)
confectioners'/icing sugar, sifted

Freeze:

Put the glasses in the freezer.

Bring the milk and the cream to a boil in a small pan. Remove from the heat and add the rosemary leaves. Leave to infuse for 10 minutes, covered. Meanwhile, rinse the limes with hot water. Finely grate the zest of the limes, and then juice them with a lemon reamer or a juicer. Pass the cream-milk mixture through a fine strainer. Add the zest and the juice of the limes, mix well and let cool in the refrigerator.

Freeze the mixture in an ice-cream maker, following the manufacturer's instructions. Fill a pastry bag fitted with a large round tip with the ice cream. Immediately fill the cold glasses with the ice cream, leaving a ¹/₂ inch (1 cm) border at the top (instead of the pastry bag to fill the glasses you can also use a spoon, but the result will not be as smooth). Reserve the ice cream in the freezer.

Meringue:

Put the egg whites and confectioners' sugar in the bowl of an electric mixer. Place the bowl in a large pan half filled with simmering water and heat the mixture until it is 120°F (50°C, warm) while beating it with a whisk. Remove the bowl from the water bath and continue to whip using the electric mixer at medium speed for 10 minutes, then at low speed for another 10 minutes to stiffen and cool the meringue. The meringue must be smooth and shiny.

Completion:

With a pastry bag fitted with a flat, plain tip pipe the cold meringue in small decorative ribbons on the ice cream. Brown the surfaces using a blowtorch and serve the ice creams immediately.

ANISE MACAROONS STUFFED WITH RASPBERRY SORBET

MACARONS À L'ANIS FOURRÉS AU SORBET DE FRAMBOISES

Serves 4

Macaroons:

(makes about 80 pieces)
2 1/4 cups plus one tablespoon
(285 g) confectioners'/icing sugar
5 ounces (160 g)
finely ground almonds
1 tablespoon (10 g)
freshly ground anise seeds
4 egg whites (120 g)

Sorbet:

1 pound (500 g) fresh raspberries
(or frozen raspberries,
if fresh are unavailable)
scant 1/2 cup (100 g) sugar
juice of a quarter of an orange
juice of half a lemon

Sauce:

3 - 4 ounces (100 g) raspberries
1 tablespoon (10 g) sugar
a few drops fresh lemon juice

To serve:

5 - 6 1/2 ounces (150 - 200 g)
of mixed berries (raspberries,
blackberries, blueberries,
strawberries)
mint leaves for garnish

Macaroons:

Preheat the oven to 400°F (200°C). Line two or three baking sheets with parchment paper. Sift together a scant 2 cups (250 g) of confectioners' sugar, the almond powder and the ground anise. Beat the egg whites until semi-firm, add the remaining 1/4 cup (35 g) confectioner's sugar, and continue to beat the egg whites until quite firm, smooth, and shiny. Delicately fold together the two mixtures until thoroughly and evenly incorporated. Using a pastry bag fitted with a plain tip, pipe small heaps of the macaroon mixture about 1 - 1 1/4 inches (2,5 to 3 cm) in diameter, onto the prepared sheets, spacing them a little.

Place one filled baking sheet into the preheated oven. Lower the temperature to 300°F (150°C) and bake the macaroons for 12 minutes without letting them color. Take the sheet from the oven and remove the macaroons by pouring a little water between the baking sheet and the paper. Let them cool for 10 minutes. Bake the remaining sheets of macaroons in the same way.

Reserve 24 of best macaroons. While they are still warm, join the remaining macaroons together in pairs. Serve these as petits fours with coffee or tea.

Sorbet:

Pick over the raspberries and mix them with the sugar and the citrus fruit juices. Pass through a fine sieve, freeze in an ice-cream maker, following the manufacturer's instructions to a creamy sorbet. Put the sorbet into a pastry bag fitted with a small plain tip and reserve in the freezer.

Sauce:

Mix the raspberries, sugar, and a few drops of lemon juice and pass through a fine sieve to obtain a smooth sauce.

To serve:

Pick over the mixed berries, rinse if necessary and halve or quarter the larger ones depending on their size. To stuff the macaroons, garnish half of the reserved macaroons, smooth sides up, with a good portion of sorbet. Cover them with remaining macaroons, press delicately and keep them until serving in the freezer.

Place three stuffed macaroons per person on cold plates. Garnish with the mixed berries, a ribbon of raspberry sauce and a mint leaf. Serve at once.

HAZELNUT PARFAIT WITH NOUGATINE
PARFAIT AU PRALIN ET À LA NOUGATINE

Serves 6 to 8

Parfait:
(to be prepared 1 day in advance)
6 to 8 soufflé molds from $^1/_2$
to $^3/_4$ cup (120 - 150 ml) capacity
$^3/_4$ cup plus
1 tablespoon (200 g) sugar
8 egg yolks (160 g)
$^1/_2$ cup plus 2 tablespoons(100 g)
hazelnut praline paste,
melted (to be bought
in a specialized cake/pastry store)
1 $^1/_2$ cups (300 g) heavy cream
candy thermometer

Nougatine:
2 $^3/_4$ ounces (85 g)
slivered almonds
7 tablespoons
(3 $^1/_2$ ounces, 110 g) sugar
neutral vegetable oil

Parfait:

Prepare your soufflé moulds: surround your molds with a wax or parchment paper band 4 inches (10 cm) high (fold the paper three times) so that you can fill the molds higher than the top edge of the molds. Fix the bands using a straight pin, then attach to the soufflé molds firmly with kitchen twine.

Combine $^1/_4$ cup plus one tablespoon of water and $^3/_4$ cup plus one tablespoon (200 g) of sugar and cook the syrup to 230°F (110°C) (check with the candy thermometer). Whip the egg yolks in the bowl of an electric mixer and gradually pour in the boiling syrup in a thin stream, whipping continually at high speed with the mixer. Continue to beat the mixture into a fine, pale yellow foam until cool. Mix some of the egg yolk mixture in with the melted praline paste, then fold that into the remaining mixture with a whisk. Whip the cream until firm. Delicately incorporate the whipped cream in thirds into the parfait mixture and divide among the prepared molds. Let the parfaits chill in the freezer at least 5 hours or, even better, overnight.

Nougatine:

Preheat the oven to 340°F (170°C).

Spread out the almonds on a baking sheet and brown slightly in the preheated oven. Melt the sugar in a small pan, and let it caramelize while stirring with a wooden spatula. Add in the almonds and pour the mixture onto an oiled baking sheet. Spread out the nougatine using an oiled icing spatula.

Let the nougatine cool completely. Break up into pieces and crush finely in a mixer or food processor. Reserve the crushed nougatine in a sealed container until needed.

To serve:

Take the parfaits from the freezer. Dust with a fine layer of nougatine, remove the collar and serve.

ROASTED PINEAPPLE WITH CHAMPAGNE ICE

ANANAS RÔTIS ET GRANITÉ DE CHAMPAGNE

Serves 4

Champagne ice:

(to be prepared 1 day in advance)
half an organic or unwaxed lemon
²/₃ cup (150 g) sugar
2 ¹/₄ cups (1/2 liter) champagne

Pineapple:

2 baby pineapples (Victoria)
2 - 3 tablespoons (40 g) butter
2 tablespoons (1 ounce, 35 g)
brown sugar
1 - 2 tablespoons (20 ml)
dark rum
¹/₂ cup (100 ml) pineapple juice
4 long wooden or bamboo skewers

Champagne ice:

Rinse the half lemon with hot water, dry it and grate the zest. Boil the sugar with 1¹/₄ cup (¹/₄ liter) of water in a pan. Add the lemon zest and let simmer a moment longer. Remove the pan from the heat and add the champagne. Let the mixture cool and pour it in a tray. Place the mixture to freeze overnight in the freezer

Pineapple:

Cut off the ends of pineapples, peel carefully and quarter lengthwise. Remove the hard core from inside the pineapple, and then cut the quarters in thick slices from ¹/₂ to ³/₄ inches (1 to 2 cm). Thread approximately 6 pieces per skewer.

Melt the butter in a large frying pan. Arrange the pineapple skewers in the pan and strew with the brown sugar. Uniformly roast them in the butter-sugar mixture until the pieces of pineapple are well caramelized. Flame them with rum and pour in the pineapple juice. Let the skewers braise a little in the sauce and then take them out of the frying pan. Reduce the cooking juices to a syrup.

To serve:

Take the champagne ice from the freezer and break up into tiny ice crystals by scraping with a fork. Fill small chilled glasses or bowls with the champagne ice.

Place the pineapple skewers on plates, remove the skewers and coat the pieces of pineapple with the cooking syrup. Serve accompanied by the champagne ice.

TRADITIONAL RUM SAVARIN
SAVARIN TRADITIONNEL AU RHUM

Makes 10 small savarins

Savarins:

*(to be prepared at least
2 days in advance)
Approximately 1 1/4 cups
(12 ounces, 200 g)
all-purpose flour, sifted
1 1/2 teaspoons (7 g) fine sea salt
1/4 ounce (8 g) fresh bakers' yeast
1 teaspoon honey
5 tablespoons (70 g) melted butter
5 medium eggs
softened butter and
flour for the molds
10 small individual savarin molds
(to be bought in a specialized
cake/pastry store)*

Syrup:

*1 3/4 cups plus 3 tablespoons
(400 g) sugar
1 vanilla bean, halved
approximately 1/2 cup
(100 ml) dark rum*

Completion:

*aged rum
1 1/2 cups (300 g) heavy cream
2 tablespoons (30 g) sugar*

Savarins:

In the bowl of an electric mixer put the flour, salt, crumbled yeast, honey, butter and an egg. Mix with the dough hook at high speed in order to obtain a rather firm but smooth dough. Add one egg after the other, working the dough 3 to 4 minutes after each addition to incorporate it well. Continue to knead the dough approximately 20 minutes until it is very elastic and shiny, and pulls away from the bowl.

Butter and flour lightly 10 savarin molds. Uniformly lay out the dough using a pastry bag fitted with a large round tip, or with your fingers, into the bottom third of the molds. Place the molds on a baking sheet slightly spaced apart. Let the dough rise in a warm place for 30 to 40 minutes, until it reaches the edge of the mold.

Preheat the oven to 350°F (180°C).

Bake the savarins approximately 20 minutes in the preheated oven. Take them out when they have a beautiful golden color. Let them cool for a moment, then unmold while still hot onto a rack. Let them dry out at room temperature for at least a day, better several days, without wrapping them (after which you can wrap them in plastic wrap and freeze them for up to 2 months).

Syrup:

Put the sugar and the split vanilla bean in a saucepan, add 1 quart/liter of water and bring to the boil. Take the pan from the heat, add rum to taste and let the syrup cool a little. Remove the vanilla pod.

Completion:

Fill a high-rimmed dish or small plate to 3/4 inch (2 cm) with the still warm syrup. Place the savarins in the syrup to soak and let soak for 5 minutes on each side so that they are soft and are soaked to the center (to check: insert the point of small knife, it should go in very easily). Take the savarins from the syrup using an offset spatula and drain on a rack set over a dish.

To serve, whip the cream until firm, adding the sugar halfway through. Fill a pastry bag fitted with a large grooved tip.

Place the savarins in soup plates, drizzle with syrup and aged rum.
Garnish them in the center by forming a rosette of whipped cream and serve.

BLACK AND WHITE CHOCOLATE MOUSSE
MOUSSE AU CHOCOLAT NOIR ET BLANC

Serves 8

Black chocolate mousse :
5 ounces (150 g) high-quality
bitter chocolate (70% cocoa solids)
1 cup (200 g) heavy cream
4 large eggs
1 scant cup (90 g) sugar

White chocolate mousse:
5 ounces (150 g)
high-quality white chocolate
1 sheet gelatin
2 tablespoons yogurt
1 cup (200 g) heavy cream
4 egg whites (4 ounces, 120 g)
1 tablespoon (10 g) sugar

Completion:
2 - 3 tablespoons unsweetened
cocoa powder

Black Chocolate mousse:
Chop the chocolate finely and melt it in a hot water bath (the bowl should not touch the water) or in a double boiler over simmering water. Separate the yolks from the egg whites. Put the egg yolks in the bowl of an electric mixer. Boil the 8 tablespoons of sugar and 3/4 cup plus 2 tablespoons (200 ml) of water approximately 2 minutes in a small pan. Pour the boiling syrup over the egg yolks, whipping them at medium speed with the mixer. Continue to beat the yolks at high speed until they double in volume and become a very pale yellow. Add the melted chocolate and let cool to room temperature. Whip the heavy cream into soft peaks, not too firm. Whip the egg whites with 1 tablespoon of the sugar into smooth, shiny, stiff peaks. First, delicately incorporate a third of the egg whites into the chocolate egg yolk mixture with a whip. Switch to a rubber spatula and fold in the remainder of the egg whites, and finally the whipped cream, in two portions. Reserve the black mousse at room temperature.

White chocolate mousse:
Chop the white chocolate finely and melt it in a hot water bath (the bowl should not touch the water) or in a double boiler over simmering water. Once the chocolate has melted, remove the bowl from the water bath. Soften the gelatin in cold water, drain well and dissolve in 2 tablespoons of boiling cream. Add the yogurt and the gelatin/cream mixture to the chocolate. Whip the heavy cream into soft peaks, not too firm. Whip the egg whites with the sugar into smooth, shiny, stiff peaks. Initially, delicately incorporate a third of the egg whites into the white chocolate with a whip. Switch to a rubber spatula and fold in the remainder of the egg whites, and finally the whipped cream, in two portions to obtain a light-textured mousse.

Completion:
Place the two mousses, alternating black and white layers, in tall cold glasses. Let each layer of mousse set in the refrigerator before adding the next to prevent them from mixing. End with a layer of the white chocolate mousse. Smooth the surface with an icing spatula and refrigerate the glasses for at least 2 hours. To serve, dust the top of the mousse with a fine layer of cocoa powder and serve immediately.

STRAWBERRY-VANILLA ICE CREAM VACHERIN
VACHERIN GLACÉ FRAISE-VANILLE

Serves 8 to 10

Meringue:
4 egg whites (4 ounces, 120 g)
1 cup (3 3/4 ounces, 120 g) sugar
1 1/4 cups (120 g)
sifted confectioners'/icing sugar

Ices:
3 cups (3/4 liter) of the custard
for vanilla ice cream (p. 175)
1 pound (500 g)
fragrant strawberries
3/4 cup (100 g) sugar
juice of a quarter of an orange
juice of a half a lemon
3/4 cup (170 g) heavy cream

Completion:
some nice small strawberries
or wild strawberries
1 1/2 cups (300 g) heavy cream
2 - 3 tablespoons (30 g)
candied violets (optional)

Meringue:

Preheat the oven to 300°F (150°C). Cover two baking sheets with parchment paper. Beat the egg whites in an electric mixer until they form stiff peaks, adding a heaping tablespoon (20 g) of sugar halfway through. Combine the two sugars together and incorporate when the whites are stiff, approximately after 5 minutes. Immediately spoon the egg whites into a pastry bag fitted with a large round tip. Squeeze out onto the baking pans, forming 3 circles 8 inches (20 cm) in diameter and 1/4 inch (1 cm) high. Place the meringues in the oven and bake them for 25 minutes at 300°F (150°C), then lower the temperature to 250°F (120°C) and continue baking for 1 1/2 - 2 hours to dry the meringue discs. They must be dry top to bottom and light golden color. Let them cool on the sheets in the turned off oven with the door slightly open.

Ice creams:

Freeze the custard for vanilla ice cream in an ice-cream maker, following the manufacturer's instructions. Pour it in a chilled container and reserve it in the freezer.

For the strawberry ice cream: pick over the strawberries, wash and hull them, and cut into pieces. Mix them with the sugar and the fruit juices into a fine purée.
Pour in the cream, and remix. Check to see if the purée is sweetened enough, and if necessary add a little more sugar. Freeze the purée in an ice-cream maker, following the manufacturer's instructions. Pour the strawberry ice cream in a chilled container and store it in the freezer.

Completion:

Pick over the wild strawberries. Whip the cream until stiff, adding the sugar toward the end. Reserve in the refrigerator. Working quickly, spread out an even 3/4 inch (2 cm) thick layer of vanilla ice cream over one disc of meringue. Smooth the surface and place the disc in the freezer until ready to assemble. In the same way, spread a second disc with the strawberry ice cream. Over the third disc, spread out one thin layer of either strawberry ice cream or vanilla, depending on what you have left.

To assemble the vacherin, place the second disc covered with strawberry ice cream on top of the disc covered with vanilla. Finish with the third disc. Smooth the edges and surface with a hot metal icing spatula and then cover with a thin layer of whipped cream. Fill a pastry bag fitted with a medium grooved tip with the remaining whipped cream. Decoratively garnish the vacherin (especially the top) with whipped cream. Freeze for fifteen minutes. To serve, decorate the vacherin with wild strawberries and violets and cut it using a hot knife into 8 to 10 portions. Serve accompanied by freshly made strawberry sauce.

MY MADELEINES
MES MADELEINES

Makes about 40 to 50

Madeleines:
*(to be prepared one day
in advance)*
*¹/2 pound plus 1 tablespoon
(250 g) butter*
*2 ¹/2 cups (9 ounces, 250 g) sifted
confectioners'/icing sugar*
8 - 9 egg whites (250 g)
*3 ¹/4 ounces (100 g)
finely ground almonds*
*6 - 8 tablespoons (75 g)
sifted flour*

Completion:
*Baking molds for madeleines
(available at high-end kitchen
supply stores)
softened butter
and flour to prepare the molds*

Madeleines:

Brown the butter in a small pan on medium heat until it has a light hazelnut odor, then remove the pan from the heat and immediately pour the butter through a fine sieve into a bowl.

Beat the confectioners' sugar lightly with the egg whites until smooth. Mix the almond powder and the flour, and add them to the sugar and egg white mixture. Pour in the warm browned butter and mix well. Let the batter rest overnight in the refrigerator covered with plastic wrap.

Completion:

Preheat the oven to 400°F (200°C).

Butter the madeleine molds with a pastry brush and flour lightly. Fill to ²/3 with the batter. Bake the madeleines 3 minutes at 400°F (200°C), then lower the temperature to 350°F (180°C) and continue to bake for approximately 4 to 5 minutes more. Take the madeleines out when they have a beautiful golden color. Let them cool for a moment and unmold while still hot. Let them cool on a rack and serve with coffee or tea.

Note:

Only bake as many madeleines as you will need for one day. They are much better eaten the day they are made. The batter will keep very well in a sealed container in the refrigerator for one week.

153

ALMOND TUILES (COOKIES)
TUILES AUX AMANDES

Makes about 40 to 50

Cookies:

6 1/2 ounces (200 g)
sliced almonds
3/4 cup plus 1 tablespoon
(6 ounces, 185 g) sugar
3 tablespoons (30 g) of sifted flour
3 - 4 egg whites .
(3 1/2 ounces, 110 g)
3 tablespoons (40 g) melted butter
a little milk

Completion:

a baking form for tuiles
(optional)

Cookies:

In a bowl, combine the almonds, sugar, and the flour well with a spatula, then add the egg whites and the warm melted butter. Place the batter in the refrigerator for 1 1/2 hour.

Completion

Preheat the oven to 350°F (180°C).

On buttered baking sheets or on sheets lined with parchment paper, form heaps of the almond batter using a tablespoon, spacing them well apart. Flatten them with a the back of a fork dipped in milk (milk adds brilliance to the cookies). The heaps must be almost flat so that the cookies cook uniformly.

Place only one pan at a time in the preheated oven and bake the cookies 8 to 10 minutes, watching carefully how much they have browned. Remove from the oven and, working quickly, remove each cookie using an offset spatula and, while still hot, place in a baking form for tuiles or drape over a rolling pin to give them their typical shape. Repeat with the rest of the almond batter. Let the cookies cool in the baking form or on the rolling pin. The cookies may be kept up to six days in a sealed container.

155

PALM TREES
PALMIERS

Makes about 60 small or 30 large

Palm trees:

6 1/2 ounces (200 g)
puff pastry dough (p. 174)
to which, following the directions
for puff pastry, you will have given
only the first double and the first
simple turn
(to be prepared the day before)
approximately 3/4 cup (80 g)
confectioners'/icing sugar

Palm trees:

Prepare the puff pastry dough the day before, giving it a double and a simple turn, as described on p. 174. Reserve in the refrigerator wrapped in plastic wrap.

Preheat the oven to 400°F (200°C). Dust your work surface abundantly with confectioners' sugar. Place the puff pastry dough on the confectioners' sugar and give it another double turn and a simple turn. Place in the freezer for 5 minutes.

Redust your work surface with confectioners' sugar and roll out the puff pastry dough in a 12 x 12 inch (30 x 30 cm) square. Cut the square into two bands 6 x 12 inches (15 x 30 cm). Fold up the pastry lengthwise to bring the two edges of each band into the center. Then close the two folds again, one against the other, to obtain 4 superimposed thicknesses of pastry.

Place the bands on a baking sheet and put them in the freezer for 5 minutes to firm them up. Slice the bands crosswise into 1/4 inch (5 mm) slices and place them flat on a baking sheet lined with parchment paper, spacing them well. Fill only one pan at the time, keeping the remaining dough in the refrigerator while the first one bakes.

Bake the palm trees approximately 10 minutes in the preheated oven until they are golden brown and crisp. Let them completely cool on a rack, stacking them only after they are cold (to prevent them from sticking to one another). The palm trees may be kept 8 days in a sealed container in a dry place.

Note:

If you want to make large palm trees, leave the square whole at the beginning, then fold as described for the small ones. The large palm trees require approximately 8 minutes longer to bake.

MARSHMALLOWS
GUIMAUVE

Makes about 2 pounds (1 kg)

Marshmallow:

6 quarter-ounce packages
gelatin (40 g) or 20 sheets
7 $^{1}/_{2}$ cups
(1 $^{1}/_{2}$ pounds, 750 g) sugar
scant $^{1}/_{4}$ cup (2 $^{1}/_{2}$ ounces, 75 g)
glucose syrup (to be bought in a
specialized cake/pastry shop)
or light corn syrup
4 egg whites (120 g)
$^{1}/_{4}$ cup (50 ml)
orange flower water
a few drops liquid red food
coloring (optional)
heaping $^{1}/_{2}$ cup (approximately
50 - 70 g) confectioners'/icing
sugar
heaping $^{1}/_{2}$ cup
(approximately 50 - 70 g)
corn starch
Candy thermometer

Marshmallows:

Cover the gelatin with cold water and allow to expand and soften (or soak the gelatin sheets in enough cold water so that they can soften). Bring the sugar, glucose syrup or corn syrup, and $^{2}/_{3}$ cup (165 ml) of water to a boil in a small pan on low heat. Continue cooking on medium heat until it reaches 260°F (127°C) (check with the candy thermometer). Start beating the egg whites into soft peaks in an electric mixer fitted with a whisk attachment. Gradually pour in the boiling syrup in a thin stream, beating the egg whites at a medium speed. Continue to beat until the meringue is semi-firm, smooth, and elastic. Drain the gelatin sheets well. Combine the gelatin with the orange flower water, and dissolve it in a medium bowl set over a pan of simmering water or double boiler while stirring. Remove the bowl from the hot water bath add a little hot meringue while mixing well with a whisk. Fold this mixture in with the remainder of the meringue, mixing well. If desired, color the meringue with a few drops of red food coloring (2 to 3 drops are enough!) to obtain a pale pink color.

Combine the confectioners' sugar with the corn starch. With this mixture, dust a small baking pan or a rectangular cake pan lined with parchment paper. Pour in the warm meringue and spread out well with an icing spatula to a depth of $^{3}/_{4}$ inch (2 cm). Smooth the surface of the marshmallow batter and dust it with the sugar-starch mixture. Let it cool.

To serve:

Detach the cold marshmallow batter from the edge of the pan using a knife blade. Unmold it on a work surface dusted beforehand with starch and confectioners' sugar. Remove the parchment paper and cut the rectangle in bands $^{3}/_{4}$ inch (2 cm) wide. Then cut into elongated diamonds. Redust the pieces of candy so that they do not stick together. The marshmallows may be kept in a sealed container in a dry spot for two weeks.

NOUGAT WITH ALMONDS AND PISTACHIOS
NOUGAT AUX AMANDES ET PISTACHES

*Makes about 3 pound
(1,3 kg) / 130 pieces*

Nougat:

(to be prepared 1 day in advance)
*1/2 cup (4 ounces, 125 g)
candied orange peel (orangeat)*
*1 1/2 cups (12 ounces, 375 g)
whole almonds*
*1 cup (8 ounces, 250 g) whole
pistachios, without skin/peeled*
*1/2 cup (6 ounces, 190 g) glucose
syrup (to be bought
in a specialty cake/pastry store),
or light corn syrup*
*1 1/2 cups plus one tablespoon
(12 ounces, 375 g) sugar*
*3/4 cup (8 ounces, 250 g)
lavender honey*
2 egg whites (60 g)
Candy thermometer

Nougat:

Preheat the oven to 280°F (140°C).

Chop the candied orange peel finely. Spread out the orange peel, almonds and pistachios on a baking sheet lined with parchment paper. Roast them for 15 to 20 minutes in the preheated oven until the nuts (pistachios and almonds) are lightly browned. Reserve, keeping warm, until the meringue is ready.

Bring the sugar, glucose syrup and 1/2 cup (120 ml) of water to the boil in a small pan over low heat. Increase the heat and boil mixture until 300°F (150°C) is reached (check with the candy thermometer). Separately heat the honey to a temperature of 275°F (135°C). Meanwhile, beat the egg whites to soft peaks in an electric mixer fitted with a whisk attachment. Initially add the boiling honey, in a thin stream, while beating the egg whites at medium speed. Then add the syrup slowly and gently. Continue to beat the mixture at low speed for 5 minutes until a compact, smooth and shiny meringue is obtained. Fold in the nuts and the orange peel using a spatula, and distribute evenly throughout the mixture. Using a wet icing spatula, spread out the hot mixture in a deep baking pan lined with parchment paper to a depth of 3/4 inch (2 cm). Let the nougat batter cool completely. Cover with plastic wrap and let harden overnight in the refrigerator.

To serve:

The following day, cut the nougat with a serrated knife crosswise into 1/2 inch (1 cm) bands and then lengthwise into 3/4 inch (2 cm) pieces.

Note:

The uncut nougat may be kept wrapped in plastic in the refrigerator for several weeks.

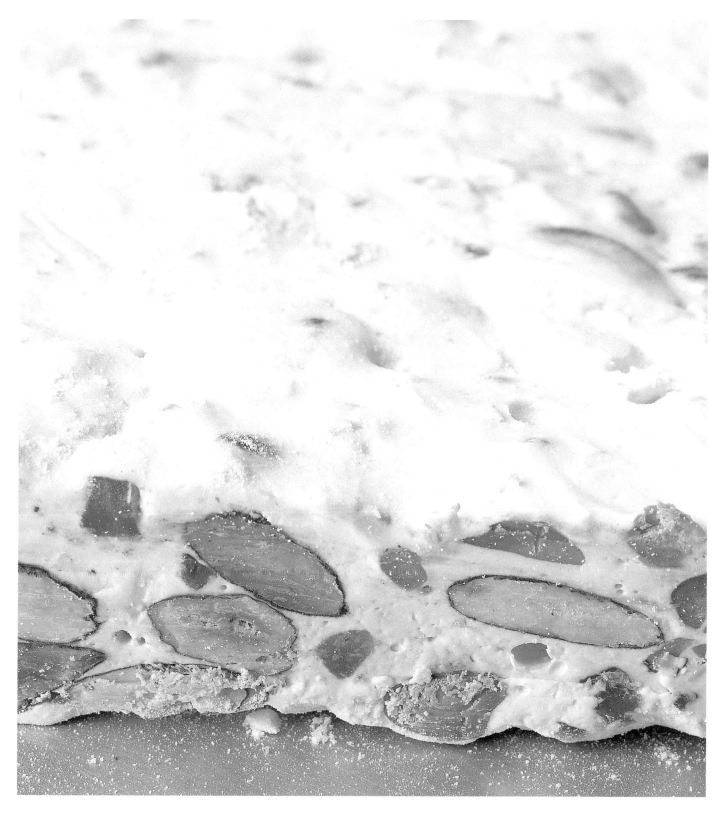

SOFT CARAMELS
CARAMELS MOUS

Makes about 250
(2 ¹/₂ pounds / 1,2 kg)

Caramels:
2 ¹/₂ cups (500g) heavy cream
2 vanilla beans, halved
1 cup (350 g) glucose syrup
(to be bought in a specialized
cake/pastry store),
or light corn syrup
1 ¹/₂ cups plus 1 tablespoon
(12 ounces, 380 g) sugar
a few drops of fresh lemon juice
2 tablespoons (30 g) salted butter
Candy thermometer

Caramels:

Heat the cream in a small pan. Using the point of a knife, scrape the seeds from the halved vanilla beans. Add the beans and their seeds to the cream. Bring to the boil. Remove the pan from the heat and let the vanilla infuse it a little. Remove the bean pods before using the cream.

Bring the glucose syrup or corn syrup, sugar, and a few drops of lemon juice to the boil in a thick-bottomed pan over medium heat while stirring with a wooden spoon. Raise the heat to high, and cook, until the syrup is amber. As soon as the color is reached, remove the pan from the heat. Add the butter in small pieces. Pour the hot cream through a fine strainer into the hot caramel while stirring constantly (be careful, the mixture can splatter!). Put the mixture back on the heat and continue cooking until the temperature reaches 240°F (116°C, check with the candy thermometer).

Pour the thick caramel on a pan covered with parchment paper. If necessary, smooth out with an oiled icing spatula to a ¹/₄ inch (1 cm) thickness. Let the caramel cool completely and cut out in ³/₄ inch (2 cm) squares.

Note:

For a beautiful presentation, wrap each caramel in a small piece of cellophane paper. The caramels may be kept in a sealed container for one week.

BRIOCHES
BRIOCHES

For 2 large brioches

Brioches:

*(to be prepared
one day in advance)*
*approximately 3 - 3 1/3 cups
(500 g)
all-purpose flour, sifted
1 ounce (20 g)
fresh baker's yeast
1 tablespoon (10 g) fine sea salt
1/4 cup (2 ounces, 60 g) sugar
6 medium eggs
1/2 pound plus one tablespoon
(250 g) butter
soft butter and flour the moulds*

Completion:

*1 egg
1 egg yolk*

Brioches:

Put the flour and crumbled yeast in the bowl of an electric mixer. Add the salt and sugar separately. Mix the eggs with 1/4 cup (50 ml) of cold water and pour them on the dry ingredients. Start to knead the mixture with the hook attachment at slow speed. Continue to knead 10 to 12 minutes at medium speed until obtaining a smooth and semi-firm dough.

While the dough is kneading, flatten butter between two pieces of waxed or parchment paper by beating it with a rolling pin to make it rather soft. When the dough is flexible and is detached from the bowl, mix again at low speed and incorporate the butter well in small pieces (if the dough is very soft, you can use the beater instead of the hook to incorporate the butter). The kneading is finished when the brioche dough is quite flexible and has a silky sheen. Then put it in a large bowl and let it rise, covered with plastic wrap, overnight in the refrigerator.

The following day, take the dough from the refrigerator. Scrape it from the bowl onto a lightly floured work surface, and divide it into two equal pieces. Shape the pieces into logs of about 10 inches (25 cm) length and place them in buttered and floured 10 inch-loaf pans. Cover them with a towel. Let them rise for 2 to 3 hours at room temperature, sheltered from drafts or in closed, turned-off oven, until they double in volume.

Completion:

Preheat the oven to 400°F (200°C). Combine the egg and the egg yolk by whipping them lightly. Glaze the risen brioches with the mixture with a pastry brush.
Bake them for 20 minutes at 400°F (200°C), then lower the temperature to 350°F (180°C) and bake for 20 minutes longer. The brioches are done when they are well risen and have a beautiful golden color. Take them from the oven, unmold them while they are still warm and let cool completely on a rack. The brioches keep for 5 days wrapped in plastic wrap or for 2 months in the freezer.

BASIC RECIPES
RECETTES DE BASE

MAYONNAISE
MAYONNAISE

Makes about 1 1/2 cups (300 g)

Ingredients:
(all of the ingredients must be
at room temperature)
2 egg yolks
1/2 teaspoon Dijon mustard
fine sea salt
1 - 1 1/4 cups (250 - 300 ml) neutral
vegetable oil (peanut or canola)
a few drops of fresh lemon juice
Cayenne pepper

Preparation:

Whisk the egg yolks, the mustard and a pinch of salt in a bowl. Allow a minute for the salt to dissolve. Initially, incorporate the oil into the egg yolks slowly, drop by drop, while constantly whisking. Gradually add the oil in a thin stream, whisking vigorously to obtain a firm but creamy mayonnaise. If the mayonnaise becomes too thick, you can add a little lemon juice. Season with Cayenne pepper and, if you want, lemon juice to taste.

Keep mayonnaise in the refrigerator until use, and consume it within the next two days.

ELEGANT VINAIGRETTE
VINAIGRETTE ÉLÉGANTE

Makes about 1 1/4 cup (250 ml)

Ingredients:
1 small shallot
6 tablespoons Ruby Port
3 tablespoons Sherry Vinegar
2 tablespoons good-quality
balsamic vinegar
fine sea salt
freshly ground pepper
1/2 cup (150 ml) neutral
vegetable oil
2 tablespoons virgin hazelnut oil
and/or 3 tablespoons of truffle juice
(speciality food stores)

Preparation:

Peel shallot and finely mince. Reduce the port in a small pan to a third (to 2 tablespoons). In a salad bowl, mix the two vinegars and a pinch of salt. Add the reduced port and minced shallot. Pour in the oil in a thin stream while whisking rapidly with a whisk. Season with pepper and salt. Scent with the hazelnut oil and/or the truffle juice. The vinaigrette can be kept tightly sealed in the refrigerator for two days.

CLARIFIED BUTTER
BEURRE CLARIFIÉ

Ingredient:

1 pound (250 g) butter

Preparation:

Melt the butter in a small pan over very low heat, without stirring, so that it separates: milk solids (whey) fall to the bottom, pure butter remains in the middle, and the impurities (white foam), which are lighter, rise to the surface. Delicately remove the foam with a spoon or fine skimmer.

Gently pass the remainder of the butter through a fine sieve covered with two absorbent paper towels, a coffee filter, or several layers of cheesecloth, stopping when you arrive at the whey. Clarified butter must have a beautiful golden color.

Note:

Clarified butter can be heated to a higher temperature than regular butter and can be kept sealed in the refrigerator for several weeks.

PARSLEY OIL
HUILE AU PERSIL

Ingredients:

1 bunch of flat-leaf parsley (approximately 2 1/2 ounces, 70 g)
sea salt
1/2 cup (80 - 100 ml) olive oil

Preparation:

Pull the leaves of the parsley from the stems. Wash and dry the leaves. Blanch them for a few seconds in salted boiling water. Shock them in ice water and drain. Press well between your hands to extract as much moisture as possible. If necessary, dry between two absorbent paper towels. In a food processor or blender mix the blanched parsley with the olive oil until the parsley is finely puréed. If still necessary, pass through a fine sieve. Salt the parsley oil just before using.

BALSAMIC VINEGAR REDUCTION
RÉDUCTION DE VINAIGRE BALSAMIQUE

Ingredient:

1 ¹/₄ cups (¹/₄ liter) good-quality balsamic vinegar

Preparation:

Reduce the vinegar in a small pan on medium heat until it has almost the consistency of a syrup. Let it cool and pour it into a plastic bottle which has a nozzle to facilitate decorating. The reduction will keep for several weeks in the refrigerator.

You can use the reduction to decorate plates or to scent sauces.

Note:

In the same way, you can carry out other reductions, for example of port or wine.

FRIED PARSLEY LEAVES
FEUILLES DE PERSIL FRITES

Ingredients:

neutral vegetable oil for deep-frying
flat-leaf parsley leaves, rather large
fine sea salt

Preparation:

Heat the oil to 325 - 350°F (160 - 170°C) in a fryer or a large frying pan.

Wash the desired quantity of parsley leaves, dry carefully and fry them
20 to 30 seconds in small batches (be careful, the oil is likely to splatter!).
When they are crispy but still green, quickly take out the leaves with a skimmer.
Drain them on absorbent paper towels. Salt lightly before using.

Note:

You can fry various kinds of leaves in the same way. For example: basil, baby spinach, or celery leaves.

SHRIMP STOCK
JUS DE CREVETTE

Makes about 1 1/4 cup (250 ml)

Ingredients:
1 onion
2 celery stalks
12 ounces (3/4 pound, 350 g)
fresh small brown shrimp
(with the heads)

Preparation:

Peel the onion and chop it finely. Clean and chop the celery stalks. Put the shrimp (not washed!) and the chopped celery and onion into a saucepan. Cover with about 2 cups (1/2 liter) of cold water. Bring to the boil and let the stock simmer for 20 minutes on low heat. Remove from the heat and let it infuse another 5 minutes. Pass the stock through a fine-meshed sieve while pressing well. According to the intensity of the taste of the stock, reduce it further in a pan (the stock must be rather strong in taste). Let it cool and then refrigerate until needed. The shrimp stock will keep, covered, for several days in the refrigerator.

FISH STOCK
FUMET DE POISSON

Makes about 4 - 5 cups (1 liter)

Ingredients:
2 pounds (1 kg) fish bones
and trimmings (form white-fleshed
fish such as flounder, sole, bass,
or snapper)
2 medium onions or 4 shallots
2 celery stalks
2 leeks
(white and light green part only)
1/2 fennel bulb
3 - 4 tablespoons (50 g) butter
1 1/4 cup (1/4 liter) dry white wine
approximately 1 1/2 quarts
(1,5 liters) cold chicken stock
(p. 172), or cold water
1 fresh thyme sprig
5 white peppercorns

Preparation:

Remove the gills from the fish heads. Chop the bones coarsely and place, with the trimmings in a large container. Rinse them under cold, running water until the water stays clear. Drain well before use.

Peel the onions or shallots and mince well. Clean the celery stalks, the white of the leek and the fennel bulb. Wash and slice them. Lightly sauté the bones and heads 4 to 5 minutes in the butter without browning. Add the vegetables and return to the heat for a few minutes. Add the white wine, let it reduce by a third and then cover with the chicken stock or water. Add the thyme and peppercorns.
Simmer for 15 minutes on low heat, removing fat and foam with a skimmer, so that it becomes quite clear.

Strain the stock through a through a fine-mesh strainer or sieve lined with a double layer of cheesecloth, without pressing. Let it cool overnight in the refrigerator. The following day degrease carefully.

The stock may be kept covered several days in the refrigerator. You can also freeze it for up to three months.

COURT-BOUILLON FOR LOBSTER
COURT-BOUILLON POUR HOMARD

Makes about 6 quarts/liters

Ingredients:

1 organic or unwaxed orange
$^1/_4$ cup (60 g) coarse sea salt
$^1/_4$ cup (20 g) dried fennel seeds

Preparation:

Using a vegetable peeler or a zester, remove the zest (outer orange part of the skin) of the orange avoiding the bitter white pith underneath. Blanch the zest for a few seconds in boiling water. Drain. In a pot place 1$^1/_2$ gallons (6 liter) of water, salt, the fennel seeds and the blanched orange zest and bring it to a boil. Cook the lobsters according to the recipe, one lobster at the time, in the simmering water.

CHICKEN STOCK
FOND DE VOLAILLE

Makes about 1$^1/_2$ quarts/liters

Ingredients:

3 pounds (1,5 kg) chicken bones
sea salt
2 onions
1 carrot
6 ounces (200 g) celery root
(celeriac)
1 leek
(white and pale green part only)
1 tomato
1 teaspoon white peppercorns
5 parsley sprigs
1 fresh thyme sprig
1 bay leaf (laurel)

Preparation:

Coarsely chop the chicken bones, rinse well under cold running water and drain. Put them in a pot and pour 2 to 2$^1/_2$ quarts (liters) cold water to cover by 1 - 1$^1/_2$ inches (2 - 3 cm). Salt the water and bring it to a boil. Skim off the foam that rises to the top as it heats. Once at the boil, lower the heat to simmer.

Meanwhile, peel the onions, carrot and celery root. Cut into $^1/_2$ to $^3/_4$ inch (1 - 2 cm) dice. Wash the leek white, dry it and slice it. Wash and coarsely chop the tomato. Add the vegetables, peppercorns, and herbs and allow the stock to simmer for 2 - 3 hours. Remove the foam several times while cooking.

Strain the stock through a fine-meshed sieve covered with a double layer of cheesecloth, pressing to extract all the juices. Let it cool overnight in the refrigerator.

The following day, degrease the stock by eliminating all the fat that has hardened on the surface. The stock may be kept covered several days in the refrigerator and freezes very well.

VEAL STOCK
FOND DE VEAU

Makes about 4 - 5 cups (1 liter)

Ingredients:

2 onions
1 carrot
6 ounces (200 g) celery root
(celeriac)
1 small leek
(white and pale green part only)
3 pounds (1,5 kg) veal bones
3 tablespoons (40 g) butter
1 teaspoon tomato paste
1 cup (1/4 liter) semi-dry white wine
2 quarts (liters) cold chicken stock
(p. 172), or cold water
1 fresh thyme sprig
1 bay leaf (laurel)

Preparation:

Peel the onions, carrot and celery root. Cut into 3/4 inch (2 cm) pieces.
Wash the leek white, dry it, and slice it. Chop the veal bones coarsely into 1 inch (3 cm) pieces (ask your butcher to do this for you).

Slowly roast the bones in butter on medium heat until they are well browned.
Add the vegetables to the bones continuing to roast for a few minutes, adding the tomato paste towards the end. Moisten with the white wine and let reduce to a syrup.
Add chicken stock to cover. Let the stock simmer on low heat for 3 to 4 hours.
If too much liquid evaporates during cooking, add in a little more stock or water.

At the end of cooking, pass the stock through a fine-meshed sieve, pressing well to extract all the juices, and let it cool overnight in the refrigerator. The following day, remove any hardened fat before using the stock. The stock can be kept several days in the refrigerator and freezes very well. You can also reduce it to a glaze and use it to enhance the taste of certain sauces and ragouts.

LAMB STOCK
FOND D'AGNEAU

Makes about 4 - 5 cups (1 liter)

Ingredients:

2 onions
1 carrot
5 ounces (150 g) celery root
(celeriac)
1 leek
(white an pale green parts only)
3 pounds (1,5 kg) lamb bones
and trimmings
3 tablespoons olive oil
1 teaspoon tomato paste
3 garlic cloves
1 fresh thyme sprig
1 bay leaf (laurel)
10 parsley sprigs
1 tablespoon black peppercorns

Preparation:

Peel the onions, carrot, and celery root. Cut into 1 inch (2 cm) pieces. Wash the leek, dry it and slice it coarsely. Chop the bones in small pieces (ask the butcher to do this). Roast the bones and the trimmings in a pot in olive oil on medium heat, turning regularly, until they well browned. Add vegetables and allow to brown too.
Add the tomato paste, stir well and cover with cold water. Add the garlic cloves, the thyme, bay leaf, parsley, and peppercorns. Let the stock simmer for 3 to 4 hours on low heat. If too much liquid evaporates during the cooking, add enough water to keep the bones covered.

After cooking, pass the stock through a fine sieve lined with two layers of cheesecloth and let it cool overnight in the refrigerator. The following day, degrease the stock carefully by eliminating the fat that has solidified on the surface.
The lamb stock may be kept covered three days in the refrigerator and three months in the freezer.

PUFF PASTRY
PÂTE FEUILLETÉE

Makes about 2¹/₂ pounds
(1,2 kg)

Ingredients:
1 pound (525 g, approximately
3¹/₂ cups) sifted flour
1 tablespoon (14 g) fine sea salt
1 pound (500 g) butter at room
temperature
flour for the work surface

Preparation:

For the first dough, put 11 ounces (350 g) of flour in the bowl of a mixer that has an attached splashguard, add 6¹/₂ tablespoons (3 ounces, 100 g) of butter in small pieces and the salt. Mix at high speed until the dough has a grainy/sandy texture. Gradually add ³/₄ cup (170 to 180 ml) cold water, and continue to mix at slow speed until the mixture forms a semi-firm dough, rather soft and smooth. Form the dough into a ball, and then roll into a square of 8 inches (20 cm) per side. Wrap it in plastic wrap and reserve it in the refrigerator for at least two hours.

For the second dough, put 13 ounces (400 g) of butter in a mixer provided with a splashguard and work the butter until it is smooth. Add 6 ounces (175 g) of flour and combine the two elements well without overworking them. Pour the dough on a large sheet of plastic wrap and form it (with a pastry scraper) into a square of 8 inches (20 cm) per side and ¹/₂ inch (1cm) thickness. Wrap it in plastic wrap and refrigerate it for two hours to firm it up.

To make the puff pastry, place the first dough on a pastry marble and roll it out into a rectangle measuring 25 x 10 inches (65 x 25 cm). Flatten the butter square (or second dough) a little by smacking it with a rolling pin, to make it less firm and place it on the larger rectangle of the first dough. Fold the two edges of the dough rectangle one after the other on the top of the butter square and press them in firmly to seal it up. Turn the pastry so that one of the open ends is facing you. Roll out the dough again into a 25 x 10 inch (65 x 25 cm) rectangle. Let it rest for half an hour in the refrigerator, covered.

For the first double turn, take the dough out of the refrigerator and fold it lengthwise by bringing the two edges of the rectangle to the center. Fold again top to bottom in order to obtain 4 superimposed thicknessess of dough (this is known as a wallet). Put the dough back in the refrigerator, covered, to rest for 30 minutes.

Take the dough out of the refrigerator and turn it so that the open end is facing you. Again roll it into a rectangle of 25 x 10 inches (65 x 25 cm) and make a simple turn (i.e.), fold in each side of the rectangle one third, one on top of the other, in order to obtain three superimposed layers). Let it rest for half an hour in the refrigerator, covered. Roll out the dough again and give it another double turn and another simple turn, letting it rest a half hour between each turn, refrigerated and covered. After the last turn, let the puff pastry rest in the refrigerator, covered, for two more hours before using it.

To use, roll out the pastry to ¹/₄ inch thickness and use it as indicated in the recipe. The puff pastry will keep, covered, for three days in the refrigerator and one month in the freezer.

PASTA DOUGH
PÂTE À NOUILLES

Makes about 1 1/2 pounds (700 g)

Ingredients:
1/2 pound (500 g) finely
milled durum wheat semolina
("semola di grando duro"
to buy in an Italian grocery)
4 - 5 eggs (depending on their size)
Flour for the work surface

Preparation:

Mix the semolina and 4 eggs in a mixer provided with a hook in order to obtain a firm and relatively hard dough. If the dough appears too dry, add another egg yolk or even a whole egg. Form the dough into a ball and wrap it well in a sheet of plastic wrap. Let it rest at least an hour or, even better, overnight in the refrigerator.

To make fresh pasta, cut the dough into four equal pieces and flatten slightly on a floured work surface. Spread each piece out individually and roll into thin bands using a pasta machine or a rolling pin. Depending on the recipe, cut the bands in squares, spaghetti or tagliatelle. Reserve the fresh pasta on a floured plate without piling them up. You can cook the pasta immediately in sufficient boiling salted water, keep it covered for up to two days in the refrigerator, or freeze it for up to one month.

VANILLA ICE CREAM
GLACE VANILLE

Makes about 1 1/2 pints (800 ml)

Ingredients:
2 vanilla beans, halved lengthwise
2 cups (1/2 liter) full-fat milk
Scant 1/2 cup (125 g) sugar
a few ice cubes
6 egg yolks
1/2 cup (100 g) heavy cream

Preparation:

With the point of a knife, scrape the small seeds from the vanilla beans. In a pan, bring the milk, the vanilla beans and their seeds, and half of the sugar to a boil. Remove the pan from the heat and let the vanilla infuse for 10 minutes, covered.

Prepare an ice bath: fill a large salad bowl with cold water and the ice cubes. Have ready a fine sieve, as well as a smaller salad bowl that will fit inside the large salad bowl, for the cream.

Beat the egg yolks with the remaining sugar in a bowl until the sugar dissolves. Pour the hot milk gradually into the sweetened egg yolk mixture while whisking well. Put the preparation in an average sized pan and heat to 185°F (85°C) (approximately 5 minutes) on low heat while whisking constantly until the mixture starts to thicken and will coat a spoon. Take the pan immediately from the heat and add the heavy cream to stop the cooking. Pour the mixture through a fine sieve into the smaller bowl and plunge that into the ice bath. Whisk the preparation from time to time while it cools.

Once it is cool, freeze the cream in an ice-cream maker, following the manufacturer's instructions. Pour the ice cream into a cold container and slip it into the freezer. If you seal it, you can keep the ice cream a few days in the freezer, but its texture is best when it is eaten on the day it is made.

INDEX OF RECIPES

(c) by Léa Linster
first edition 2003
ISBN 2-9599-854-2-7

Editor: Léa Linster
Texts and recipes: Simone van de Voort
Translation French-English: Chip Browder
Culinary advisers: Hàkon Màr Orvarsson, Dominique Simonnet,
Thierry Ouvrard
Black and white photographs: Susie Knoll
Photographs: Guy Hoffmann
Artistic Direction: Paul Zentner
Graphics: Lambert Herr, Michele Zeyen
Printing: saint-paul, Luxembourg